Defiant
JOY

Also by Stasi Eldredge

Captivating
Love and War
Becoming Myself
Free to Be Me

Defiant
JOY

TAKING HOLD OF HOPE,

BEAUTY, AND LIFE IN A HURTING WORLD

STASI ELDREDGE

NELSON
BOOKS

An Imprint of Thomas Nelson

Published in Nashville, Tennessee, by Nelson Books, an imprint of Thomas Nelson. Nelson Books and Thomas Nelson are registered trademarks of HarperCollins Christian Publishing, Inc.

Published in association with Yates & Yates, www.yates2.com.

Thomas Nelson titles may be purchased in bulk for educational, business, fund-raising, or sales promotional use. For information, please email SpecialMarkets@ThomasNelson.com.

Unless otherwise noted, Scripture quotations are taken from the Holy Bible, New International Version®, NIV®. Copyright © 1973, 1978, 1984, 2011 by Biblica, Inc.® Used by permission of Zondervan. All rights reserved worldwide. www.Zondervan.com. The "NIV" and "New International Version" are trademarks registered in the United States Patent and Trademark Office by Biblica, Inc.®

Scripture quotations marked ESV are from the ESV® Bible (The Holy Bible, English Standard Version®). Copyright © 2001 by Crossway, a publishing ministry of Good News Publishers. Used by permission. All rights reserved.

Scripture quotations marked KJV are from the King James Version. Public domain.

Scripture quotations marked THE MESSAGE are from *The Message*. Copyright © by Eugene H. Peterson 1993, 1994, 1995, 1996, 2000, 2001, 2002. Used by permission of NavPress. All rights reserved. Represented by Tyndale House Publishers, Inc.

Scripture quotations marked NASB are from New American Standard Bible®. Copyright © 1960, 1962, 1963, 1968, 1971, 1972, 1973, 1975, 1977, 1995 by The Lockman Foundation. Used by permission. (www.Lockman.org)

Scripture quotations marked NKJV are from the New King James Version®. © 1982 by Thomas Nelson. Used by permission. All rights reserved.

Scripture quotations marked NLT are from the *Holy Bible*, New Living Translation. © 1996, 2004, 2007, 2013, 2015 by Tyndale House Foundation. Used by permission of Tyndale House Publishers, Inc., Carol Stream, Illinois 60188. All rights reserved.

Scripture quotations marked RSV are from Revised Standard Version of the Bible. Copyright 1946, 1952, and 1971 National Council of the Churches of Christ in the United States of America. Used by permission. All rights reserved.

Any Internet addresses, phone numbers, or company or product information printed in this book are offered as a resource and are not intended in any way to be or to imply an endorsement by Thomas Nelson, nor does Thomas Nelson vouch for the existence, content, or services of these sites, phone numbers, companies, or products beyond the life of this book.

ISBN 978-1-4002-0869-2 (TP)
ISBN 978-1-4002-0870-8 (eBook)

Library of Congress Cataloging-in-Publication Data

Names: Eldredge, Stasi, author.
Title: Defiant joy : taking hold of hope, beauty, and life in a hurting world / Stasi Eldredge.
Description: Nashville : Thomas Nelson, 2018.
Identifiers: LCCN 2018015732 | ISBN 9781400208692
Subjects: LCSH: Joy--Religious aspects--Christianity.
Classification: LCC BV4647.J68 E43 2018 | DDC 248.8/6--dc23 LC record available at https://lccn.loc.gov/2018015732

Printed in the United States of America
18 19 20 21 22 LSC 10 9 8 7 6 5 4 3 2 1

For Jesus,
the fount and future of all joy.
It's all for You.

*And those the L*ORD *has rescued will return.*
They will enter Zion with singing;
everlasting joy will crown their heads.
Gladness and joy will overtake them,
and sorrow and sighing will flee away.

—ISAIAH 35:10

Contents

Introduction xi

Chapter 1: A Holy Defiance 1

Chapter 2: The Cup 15

Chapter 3: Whiplash 33

Chapter 4: Interference 53

Chapter 5: Greener Grass 67

Chapter 6: A Divine Exchange 83

Chapter 7: Expectant 97

Chapter 8: Thieves That Come 117

Chapter 9: The Signs All Around Us 137

Chapter 10: Cultivating Joy 151

Chapter 11: On Behalf of Love 171

Chapter 12: A Hui Hou 185

Daily Prayers 201

Acknowledgments 211

About the Author 215

Notes 217

Introduction

Why *Defiant Joy?* Why not read a book simply on joy? The answer is an easy one. In this world where we find ourselves living, having joy often feels both crazy and out of reach. That's why the title of this book includes the word *defiant*. Defiant means to stand against the tide. It means to go against the flow, even when the flow is composed of a strong current of despair and difficulty.

To have joy in the midst of sorrow—or the current news feed—can seem impossible. And all on our own, it *is* impossible. But just as the angel Gabriel said after making his outlandish proclamation to Mary that she, a virgin, would give birth to the Savior of the world, "Nothing will be impossible with God" (Luke 1:37 NASB).

Joy is meant to be ours, a joy that is defiant in the face of this broken world. Our hearts are to echo the heartbeat of our joyous God. Now, this isn't about skipping around in the garden singing, "I'm so happy in Jesus every day." This is about being present to whatever may be coming our way and, in the midst of both the goodness and the grief, knowing joy.

Believing that sorrow and loss do not have the final word takes defiance. It requires a strength of spirit that must be nurtured. It means engaging our lives fully but interpreting them by the highlight of heaven. Denying the truth of reality is not the answer; being fully present to it is.

The invitation from God to "rejoice, again I say rejoice"[1] comes to us in the middle of our lowest lows as well as our highest highs. How do we do that? Let's find out together.

One

A Holy Defiance

Joy is the serious business of Heaven.
—C. S. LEWIS

It is a quiet morning. The house is empty save for our two resigned dogs—resigned because they sense this master will not be taking them on a walk anytime soon. They know it from my slow movements, which cause their natural exuberance to dim. This morning, I will not allow myself to be baited by their soft, desire-filled eyes. *Sorry, guys. The bed is just too cozy, and it's my day off.*

Suddenly the quiet is broken as my youngest golden, Maisie, still a puppy by every standard, dashes from my bedside and begins to bark indignantly. I can guess the reason. It is the bark she uses to alert all within earshot that some neighboring cow has trespassed onto her property. Looking out my bedroom window, I see a confused little black bovine, backside still raw with the telltale signs of a too-new brand, wandering along our side of the fence. Our offended dog will let this calf, separated from her lumbering mother, know her mistake. There will be no reunions on Maisie's front porch.

In the peace that returns after Maisie calms down, having barked the calf on her way, I notice the air smells of smoke. It is the height of summer now: fire season. There is a fire burning somewhere close. Too close.

The smell of smoke used to be one I liked. It is reminiscent of campfires and conversations, marshmallows when I was young. Now, though, I am too closely acquainted with forest fires. We've lived through three fires since moving to Colorado, but the Waldo Canyon fire that swept through Colorado in 2012, burning 347 homes and swallowing 18,000 acres of gorgeous forest, had come the closest. The hungry flames came within twenty feet of our house. The courageous firefighters and Vandenberg Air Force Base "Hot Shots" gave it up for lost, taking their stand across our street against the raging inferno. We evacuated in speed, shock, and tears, and for long minutes we did not know if we would live or die, swallowed up by flames ourselves. No. I no longer find the fragrance of smoke comforting.

Flames are licking all around us, aren't they? All the time. Saint Peter describes our life here on this earth as a "fiery ordeal" (1 Peter 4:12). Tragedies and heartache and pressures and illnesses and irritations grand and small show up indiscriminately, and they do not limit themselves to one season. I become very sick, but my husband becomes much more ill at the same time—and my children hit a crisis and the call comes telling us of a loved one dying and the letter arrives from the IRS telling us we are going to be audited and the plea for help arrives in our inbox from a friend because her son is suicidal and the deadline for a project is pending and another friend has found a lump in her breast, and all this occurs within two days.

Life is hard, and it doesn't seem to let up.

I know that in comparison to most, my own life has not been so bad. I am not a refugee. I am not living in the middle of a drought-filled land, praying that my child will survive another day. My daily reality is not set in a war zone (well, at least not one that can be seen). I am not living on the streets. I have a roof over my head. I have running water that will not make me ill. When I put my feet on the floor after a night's sleep, there is carpet underneath them. I am a resident of the United States and living a life of luxury in comparison to 90 percent of the human population. I'm very aware of all this.

But such facts, though true and humbling, don't help me most of the time. Too often they serve only to shame me and keep me from being present to the sorrow in my life that threatens to swallow up everything, like a forest fire that looms near. Too near. Yes, I want to be aware of others in the world. I do want to grow in compassion, but that will require me to feel my own pain, to not run from it through comparisons that only serve to diminish my own hard. When I do not have compassion for myself in my own trials, my compassion for others also goes down—both for those whose sorrows I have known in part and those whose sorrows I have not. Besides, the grace of God is not present in my comparisons. It is here for me in my moment. If I run from my reality, I also run from the presence of God.

So my heart scans the horizon in the quiet of the morning when the faint smell of smoke rises, and I ask, "Where are You, God?"

And the answer comes from deep within. "I'm right here."

Defiance, Not Denial

Our home had been overtaken by fairy lights. Christmas twinkle lights, boughs of evergreens, ribbons of red, and the fragrance of pine filled the living room. It was the night of our annual Christmas party, and I was ready. I'd been decorating for weeks. Even the bathroom had a little sleigh in it.

Once a year our team gathers in our home to celebrate all that God has done through our little ministry. We reflect. We give thanks. We feast. We laugh. And we get all dressed up to do it. Plus, it's catered, so there's that. It's planned two months in advance, and as it draws near the expectation of joy rises exponentially.

That year, I had a spare moment on the afternoon of the party before I needed to get dressed, so, as is often the case, I went online to check out what was happening in the world. Take a look at emails. Update my Facebook status.

When I did, I learned what had transpired that day and wept with shock and despair. My soul was filled with anger and deep sorrow.

A lone gunman had opened fire on elementary school–aged children, killing twenty six- and seven-year-olds in a terrifying and horrific spree. Six adult staff were also shot and killed. It was the deadliest shooting at any school in the United States. After brutally taking these precious lives, the gunman had committed suicide.[1]

I found my husband and told him of the tragedy. We wept and prayed together. Then, as we thought about all the people who were about to show up at our house, we wondered, *How could we celebrate life in the face of such wickedness and loss?*

And that's when the phrase "defiant joy" was born. We would not cancel the party. We would gather. We would not pretend that the shootings had not taken place, nor would we forget that a whole community was grieving the children lost, but we would proclaim that even so, *even so*, there was a reason to celebrate—particularly since it was Christmastime, when we gather to honor and remember the invasion of the kingdom of God. That's what Christmas is, you know. It's an *invasion*.

The battle between good and evil could not have been made starker on that day, and it looked like a victory for the kingdom of darkness. But we needed to remember that Jesus had entered the darkness and brought the light. His unending life signaled the end to the rule of evil and proclaimed the ultimate victory of the kingdom of God. Yes, a battle was raging, but Jesus had won it, and we were invited to proclaim it and enforce it.

Once everyone had gathered in our home that night, we paused and prayed and, in silence, honored the lives lost and the families forever changed. And then we turned our hearts to the One who is our hope in the face of loss and untold grief. Because of Jesus—His death, His resurrection, and His ascension—we chose to honor Him and celebrate that He has won and is winning still.

We feasted. We talked long into the night by candlelight and Christmas music. We lingered in one another's presence, drawing closer to the fire of each other's hearts than we might otherwise have done *because* of the pain. We were defiantly joyful.

Defiant joy is different from mere defiance. And it is completely other than denial.

———

April 26, 2001, 11:00 a.m. My mother had just died. Her passing was a holy one. My sisters, aunt, and I were gathered around her bed in her home, singing her into eternity. It was a precious and sacred time, made even more so by our sharing it together. At 1:00 p.m., the somber, respectful men in their dark suits came with a stretcher to take her body away. It was at this moment that the reality of our loss hit one of my sisters and hit her hard. She needed more time with my mother. Years of being physically and emotionally distant caught up with her. Now she refused to let the chagrined men do their work. They eventually had to leave empty-handed.

That turned out to be okay, though, because it allowed time for my aunt to take pictures. It must be a North Dakota thing. An old-world thing. I don't know. It's not my thing. My aunt carefully placed flowers around my mother's lovely departed self and snapped away. When forty-five photos of my dead mother arrived a month later, I wasn't quite sure what I was supposed to do with them. Frame one?

Hours after the terrified funeral workers left, they returned, stretcher again in hand. My sister would have none of it. The rest of us thought we might have to resort to drugs. Or a straitjacket. Whether those devices would be for her or for us, we weren't sure.

A body without the spirit does not linger well. My mother's body needed to be lent into the care of others. Fortunately my brother was in the house. Strong. Firm. Determined. And angry. He had chosen not to view my mother's body after she had passed on to her forever home, but my sister's pain forced him to. He had to go into my mother's bedroom and convince my sister to let her go.

It was with sorrow, with unabsorbed grief, and with a camera snapping that I stood by as they finally wheeled my mother's body past.

What is one to do after such a moment but acquiesce to my aunt's offer to go get some dinner?

Okay. You betcha. Super. Besides, she had already chosen the restaurant.

In shell shock, we all piled into her car as she drove us to a teppanyaki restaurant. Do you know the kind I'm talking about? It's the one where diners gather around a common table while the chef awes the guests with his prowess with cutlery. Up in the air goes the zucchini. Down come the chopped spirals. I had no words.

There we were, reeling from the trauma not only of my mother's passing but from my sister's heart-wrenching grief, and we were supposed to be cheering for an onion volcano. Suffice it to say, we were not the chef's best audience that night.

I tell you this story in its somewhat macabre humor as an illustration of denial. Going to a festive dinner that night was very different from our Christmas celebration years later. One was honest, somber, and present both to the reality of the day and the reality of eternity, and the other was numbing and dishonoring, increasing our sorrow by diminishing it. We don't want to live in denial. We want to embrace defiant joy.

The evening after my mother's passing was simply not a time for cheering; it was a time for weeping. It was a time to allow our hearts the quiet, the rest, and the repose they needed to begin to absorb the loss. Beauty would have helped. A quiet walk in the woods or along the shore would have been good. But instead we got blades, flames, and suppression of the sorrow filling our hearts. Trying to diminish the pain only increased its potency.

Ignoring reality does not breed joy. Pretending that what is true does not exist is not holy defiance. The seeds of joy can only be firmly planted in the pungent soil of the here and now while at the same time being tethered to eternity. Joy is fully rooted in the truth. Joy embraces all the senses and is fully awake to the laughter, the wonder, and the beauty present in the moment as well as the sorrow, the angst, and the fear. Joy says, "Even so, I have a reason to celebrate."

Crazy, right? Sounds like God. A God who laughs at the sneers of the enemy, stares suffering in the face, and proclaims with fierce love, "You do not have the final word." And as He does, He captures our deep hearts with a hope that defies death.

Defiant may not be a word we would normally associate with the living God, but it can actually be quite fitting. Defiance means resistance, opposition, noncompliance, disobedience, dissent, and rebellion. And when it comes to things that would destroy our souls, that is exactly the right response.

We are called to resist the lies of the enemy. Like Christian in *Pilgrim's Progress*, we do not comply with the Vanity Fair offerings of the world. We are instructed not to obey the clamoring of the flesh. We are urged to rebel against sin. By the life of Christ in us, we oppose death and destruction. We dissent by casting our vote against the belief that sorrow and endless suffering win.

Instead we welcome life, love, and the full work of Christ to bring all of His goodness into every aspect of our and His domains. We comply with truth. We obey our God. We respect His authority and His final say. We overcome evil with good. We defy hatred by embracing love.

We choose joy.

In the midst of all the suffering in the world, it can feel irresponsible, even frivolous, to have joy. And yet, and still, we are called to it. Certainly there is a time to grieve. There is a time to mourn. To wail. To sigh. There is a time to know our loss and not have to cheer the teppanyaki chef, but that doesn't mean we can't have joy even in that painful knowing. Joy is the heartbeat of the kingdom of God. Joy is what sustains us; it is our strength. We can be resilient. We can be filled with the expectation of good things.

And we can have joy in the midst of the lamentations of our lives.

Joy, Not Happiness

What exactly does it mean, though, to have joy? I think we know instinctively that joy is different from happiness. Both are great. But joy seems higher, doesn't it? Better somehow. Rooted in more reliable things.

Happiness is circumstantial. I'm happy when I wake up and realize it's not Monday but Saturday—I have a day off! I'm happy when someone brings me a cup of coffee. I'm happy when I get a birthday card. I'm sad when a vacation is over. I'm sad when I mishandle the heart of a friend. I'm sad when no one remembers my birthday.

I love being happy. But happiness is unpredictable; it feels vulnerable because it is tied to my circumstances. And don't we all know it. One day you're up; next day you're down. Circumstantial happiness is an emotional roller coaster; it can really take you for a ride. It makes us heartsick in the way rolling seas and careening decks make us seasick.

Joy is something else altogether. It feels firmer, richer, less vulnerable somehow. I'm happy when my family goes out for ice cream, but it seems a little overblown to say I was filled with joy because of it. I was joyful at the weddings of my three sons. I was filled with joy over the birth of our granddaughters. Joy flooded my heart when a dear friend was cleared of cancer. I don't think it was merely happiness; the joy felt rooted in the presence of God. His hand was so evident.

Joy is *not* happiness on steroids. It is not happiness squared. Every healthy human being has the capacity to feel happiness, but joy is something entirely different, made up of its own unique substance. It doesn't come with the price of admission. Joy is connected to God and reserved for those who are tapping into His reservoir, who are connected to His life.

Joy is rooted in God and His kingdom, in the surety of His goodness, His love for us. It is immovable. Unshakable. Joy is available at all times, day and night, because God and His kingdom are always available to us. I'm ready to get off

11

the roller coaster of happiness; I want my heart grounded in the higher place of joy. I bet you do too.

Who among us does not want more joy in our lives? In our work. In our marriages. In our relationships. With our children. In our quiet moments alone. If joy is a fruit of the Spirit (and it is), then we are meant to experience and enjoy it, regardless of our circumstances. Whatever may be swirling around us, the eye of the storm is joy. But how do we get there? The simple answer is we need to come to know God more deeply. When we do, we can believe and rest in His faithful, immovable, immeasurable love for us in every moment we are in.

Joy *is* the heartbeat of heaven, the very light that emanates from Jesus' heart, so as we grow closer in relationship with God, we'll also grow in joy. We'll see that He is not spending His moments wringing His hands, as we are sometimes prone to do. He is not braced against the future or overcome by serious hardship. His joy is never up for grabs. Rather, His joy is immovable, just as He is. It is an essential part of His very person.

Thirteenth-century mystic and poet Meister Eckhart wrote:

Do you want to know what goes on in the heart of the Trinity?

I will tell you.

In the heart of the Trinity the Father laughs and gives birth to the Son.

The Son laughs back at the Father and gives birth to the Spirit.

The whole Trinity laughs and gives birth to us.[2]

We are born from the laughter of the Trinity. What an amazing thought. As image bearers of the Living God, surely joy is written deep in our very hearts. So it should come naturally, right?

Time for a confession. I am not a naturally joyful person. My battle in life has not been needing to be pulled back into reality because of my Pollyanna worldview. My battle has been with depression, ranging from debilitating to a mental-health low-grade fever; the struggle to get out of bed in the morning is one I am acquainted with. I know what it feels like to spend your days walking through sludge up to your knees with a heavy cloak on your back. But I also know the incredible feeling of having it replaced with a sense of hope and promise leading to a deep, untouchable joy. I'm learning. I do want to get off the emotional roller coaster of circumstantial happiness. I do want to be rooted and grounded in joy. Sometimes, though, it takes more intentionality to pursue it in our lives. Sometimes it's hard to take hold of. But it's worth it.

That's what I'm after. That's what I believe God is calling us to. It's what I am calling us to as well.

Two

The Cup

*Dear children, let us not love with words
or speech but with actions and in truth.*
—1 JOHN 3:18

Sometimes I feel as though I am standing outside my own life, looking through a plate-glass window that I cannot pass through. On the other side are those I love. I watch my husband and sons play with a freedom and ease of soul that is foreign to me. Their "otherness"—no, *my* otherness—weighs my heart down, frequently making it impossible for me to enter into their joy.

My immediate family is a close one. My husband and

I, together with our sons and their wives, can talk honestly about matters of the heart. Difficult subjects need to be handled with care, but we are committed to the dialogue because we are committed to one another. And yet, so frequently, though loved and loving, I feel like an island set apart from their land of mystery.

I have also been on the other side of the plate-glass window from other women, noticing as they share glances and inside jokes of connection and friendship and wondering at their intimacy. Friends respond to invitations on Facebook to parties I was not party to. People speak of movies and books they love that I have tried to watch or read but, too often, after the first few minutes have shaken my head in dismay and walked away. I do not share many, oh so many, of my friends' and family's experiences.

I don't fit.

I'm outside.

Something must be bent and broken within me.

With my male family (even our pets are boys), I thought perhaps it was my femaleness, my estrogen an unknown entity to their overflowing testosterone. It was easier to think that. When my sons were younger, I thought perhaps it was my brokenness, my shame, or my being out of shape that prevented me from belonging to them in the way I perceived them belonging to each other. But as the years have passed and circumstances have changed, I still feel that unexplainable otherness.

I recently shared this with my husband and sons, about

so frequently feeling like an outsider to my world, to them, even to myself. They nodded their heads, eyes filled with shared self-recognition. I was surprised to realize that they, too, were acquainted with that feeling in the different phases of their own lives.

In *A Tale of Two Cities*, Charles Dickens wrote that the people who teemed within the cacophony of London shared this feeling: "A wonderful fact to reflect upon, that every human creature is constituted to be that profound secret and mystery to every other."[1]

Oh. It isn't just me. It isn't just you either. Feeling "other," feeling "apart," feeling that we don't "quite fit" is the human condition. Loneliness isn't lonely. After gently unearthing a person's heart from the protective surface surrounding it, I have yet to meet one person who does not confess to loneliness.

We humans are a mystery. We are not meant to be a stranger unto our very selves, but feeling like a stranger in our world, even to those closest to us, is often a commonplace experience.

Feeling alone is a sorrow we share, and being alone is the first thing God named as "not good": "It is not good for the man to be alone" (Gen. 2:18). Yet we do feel alone. Isolated. Not understood and too often not wanted. It is not merely your condition; it is one we all have, and one that we feel compelled to run from. Numb. Escape. Ignore. It is a difficult thing to long for connection and meaning and live under a burden of futility and an emptiness that mocks. But when we run, we seed the fruit of denial and end up increasing our pain rather than soothing it. Hopelessness and denial may temporarily deaden desire and the pain of when it is unmet, but desire is a flame that refuses to be quenched.

Trying to do so never works and instead can too easily lead to damaging addictions.

As John Eldredge and Brent Curtis wrote in *The Sacred Romance*:

> Whatever the object of our addiction is, it attaches itself to our intense desire for eternal and intimate communion with God and each other in the midst of Paradise—the desire that Jesus himself placed in us before the beginning of the world. Nothing less than this kind of unfallen communion will ever satisfy our desire or allow it to drink freely without imprisoning it and us. Once we allow our heart to drink water from these less-than-eternal wells with the goal of finding the life we were made for, it overpowers our will, and becomes, as Jonathan Edwards said, "like a viper, hissing and spitting at God" and us if we try to restrain it.[2]

We have an ache. It is a valid one. Of course we long to be endlessly loved; we are made in the image of a God who is endlessly loving. We ache with desire because we are meant for a life that is not yet ours. We try to escape the sorrow out of fear that the sorrow will smother whatever hope of happiness remains. We run to a quick fix because we know our hearts need fixing.

The full list of happy quick fixes available would fill a book. Dopamine, serotonin, oxytocin, and endorphins are the quartet of neurotransmitters that make you feel happy, God bless them. Getting a text on your phone releases dopamine, and so does just looking at it. Maybe you were wondering why some people admit to feeling glued to their cell phones. It provides a happy jolt. So does sugar. So does alcohol. The list is long, and some of the items on it bear the potential for much more harm than others.

I love feeling happy. Absolutely love it. Who doesn't? But my pursuit of it has sometimes gotten me into trouble. I'm pretty sure it's gotten you into trouble too.

Sometimes I wonder if, in our mad pursuit of happiness, we run right past the joy that might be ours. We work hard to change our circumstances or change ourselves so that we might be happy. We get ourselves into addictive behaviors (exercise, by the way, is also very addicting; so is organizing your life). Then we work hard to get ourselves out of our addictions, which sometimes only makes matters worse. And all the while, God is right beside us with a gentle invitation to joy. But we can't hear that invitation while we are focused on whatever it is we think has to happen in order to make us happy.

If we want to live in the power of Jesus' resurrection, we must first pass through the crucifixion. We must stop running. Self-soothing may last for a moment, but that moment may become a doorway to a cell. Jesus came to set us free, and in Him we can be. But we will not be free if we continue to hide and refuse to face the bitter sorrow that must be braved in order to bear goodness.

Suffering is an essential part of all our lives. And it is when we are in the very midst of it that God reminds us that the absence of suffering is not our good. The presence of God is our good. And knowing His presence in the pain is the sweetest gift of all.

And Then There's Paul

In the short book of Philippians—only four chapters long—Paul uses the word *joy* sixteen times.[3] Paul didn't write this book during spring break. He wrote it from a prison cell in Rome while he was waiting to be executed. In what should have been the darkest days of his life, he wrote the most encouraging book in the Bible.

Paul did not write from a position of denial but from a position of sober and joyful reality. Right there in his chains, he wrote about "the surpassing worth of knowing Christ Jesus my Lord, for whose sake I have lost all things" (Phil. 3:8). Paul knew something; he *experienced* something. The word he uses here to describe his experience—his knowing—isn't theoretical. It's not knowing like you might know about the ancient Sumerians or the law of thermodynamics. The word is *gnosis*, a deep, personal, intimate knowledge. Paul had experienced God in such a way that even in jail he could find a very real joy as he fixed his gaze on Jesus.

He wasn't faking it either; he wasn't living in some form of spiritualized denial. Here in his treatise on joy he speaks honestly of his sufferings (Phil. 1:29–30). He later describes being "poured out like a drink offering" (2 Tim. 4:6). Paul wrote his letters with an indisputable hope that burned all the brighter because he didn't deny his suffering.

Whatever else this means, it tells us that joy is available no matter our circumstance. Good heavens—Jesus went to the *cross* with a view of joy before Him (Heb. 12:2). As the psalmist wrote, "Weeping may stay for the night, but rejoicing comes in the morning" (Ps. 30:5). This isn't the Christian bait-and-switch. This isn't for "someday." No. Joy is promised now, and it is our inheritance. There is a way to joy. The key is walking that way with our gaze set on Jesus, even when the way is dotted with suffering.

The Great Debate

Everyone is trying to find their way to joy, and if not joy, at least happiness. That's a good desire, by the way: It fuels our search. It keeps us moving forward. Folks who give up even *wanting* to be happy are deep into what might be called depression.

But in Christendom there seems to be this perennial debate about how to get there. One camp, rising in popularity for obvious reasons, promises a life above and beyond suffering. If we just worship/believe/proclaim/whatever, we can live in the fullness of the kingdom of God right now! We don't have to be sick/poor/hurting. Victory is ours! There is a way around the suffering!

The other camp—often in reaction to these bold claims—tries very hard to say that no, the promises of God are mostly for later. The healing, the breakthrough, the victory is later. After you die. In heaven. Some of the advocates of this position are very, very dear saints, who, unable to find breakthrough, have made a theology of their own disappointment.

I just want to point out two things: First, suffering is guaranteed to the saints. Jesus says to the disciples and to us, "In this world you will have trouble" (John 16:33). Second, joy is clearly promised to the children of God *in this life*. Jesus said to His disciples, "Until now you have asked for nothing in My name; ask and you will receive, so that your joy may be made full" (John 16:24 NASB).

It's not an either/or situation, thank God. Because, as much as many of us have tried, we don't seem to be able to rid the world of suffering just by worshipping longer or praying harder or whatever the magic method is supposed to be. I believe a great deal of breakthrough and healing *is* available in this life. The history of the church is filled with such stories. I also believe joy and breakthrough are not opposed to suffering but are available in the midst of it. Suffering is not a failure of faith on our part; its presence does not mean the absence of the promises of God. We can live with suffering and joy simultaneously. How does this work?

Joy is deeply rooted in the availability of God and His kingdom right here, right now. Sometimes we find breakthrough. Sometimes we find a deeper knowing of God in our suffering. But neither breakthrough nor suffering is ultimately the point. The joy that Paul discovered, the joy that Jesus knew and invited us into, begins in a deeper experience of God, whatever our situation might be.

Jesus and the Cup

As we consider what it looks like to find joy in suffering, there is no higher example than that of Jesus Himself. Let's take a closer look at His final days on earth.

In 1 Corinthians 11:24–26, Paul recounted Jesus' words from the Last Supper with His disciples: "In the same way, after supper he took the cup, saying, 'This cup is the new covenant in my blood; do this, whenever you drink it, in remembrance of me.'"

This is when the imagery of the cup first appears. Interestingly, it continues to show up as the night went on. When Jesus and His disciples left the supper, they went to the Garden of Gethsemane, and Jesus mentioned the cup again:

Going a little farther, he fell with his face to the ground and prayed, "My Father, if it is possible, may *this cup* be taken from me. Yet not as I will, but as you will." (Matt. 26:39, emphasis added)

He went away a second time and prayed, "My Father, if it is not possible for *this cup* to be taken away unless I drink it, may your will be done." (Matt. 26:42, emphasis added)

He left them and went away once more and prayed the third time, saying the same thing. (Matt. 26:44)

"Not My will," Jesus said, "but Your will be done, Father." After asking God to take away the cup three times but ultimately putting it in His Father's hands, Jesus continued down the path to His coming sacrifice:

It wasn't long before a mob entered among the olive trees, searching for Jesus. They were, of course, being led by one of Jesus' closest friends—one who had just enjoyed the final meal with Him. Jesus felt the cold, black kiss of betrayal as Judas's lips brushed His cheek. He felt the ropes and chains wrap around Him as His freedom was taken. He heard the racing footsteps of the last of His friends as they abandoned Him. Jesus was completely and utterly alone.

What makes this scene so moving and tragic is that we probably each have stories of betrayal, isolation, and abandonment that we can relate to. We know to some degree what this feels like. And this is our God we're speaking of—a human God abandoned, betrayed, and isolated by those He created.[4]

When the soldiers came to the garden and Jesus stepped forward to offer Himself to His enemies, Peter also stepped forward and cut off the ear of the high priest's servant. Jesus scolded Peter and told him to put away his sword. Then He asked, "Shall I not drink the cup the Father has given me?" (John 18:11).

What is this cup? Actually, Jesus had mentioned this cup prior to that fateful night.

Earlier, in Matthew 20:20–28, the mother of James and John, in typical motherly fashion, asked Jesus whether her nice, upstanding sons could have the honor of sitting beside Him in His kingdom. Jesus answered with a question: "Are you able to drink the cup that I am about to drink?" (Matt. 20:22 NASB).

It was not a rebuke. It was simply a question, to which the brothers replied, "We are able" (Matt. 20:22 NASB).

It was a yes blithely given. Clearly they couldn't understand the full weight of what Jesus was asking. Jesus then turned to the other disciples who were mad that James and John's mother had presumed to ask such a thing. They wanted to be seated next to Jesus as well.

Jesus spoke to all of them then and said that greatness in the kingdom of God is not easily obtained. It comes along the path of love—a path of sacrifice, service, and suffering. This is the cup of Jesus. And the people who seek to follow in His footsteps must drink of it and become like the one who came "not . . . to be served, but to serve, and to give his life as a ransom for many" (Matt. 20:28).

Can We Drink That Cup?

Let's take a deeper look into the fullness of what this cup means. Where else in the Bible have we seen the imagery of the cup? There are several passages that connect God's wrath with the cup. Jeremiah 25:15 tells us, "Thus the LORD, the God of Israel, said to me: 'Take from my hand this *cup* of the wine of wrath, and make all the nations to whom I send you drink it'" (ESV, emphasis added). Then, in Isaiah 51:17 it says, "O Jerusalem, you who have drunk from the hand of the LORD the *cup* of his wrath" (ESV, emphasis added). In Revelation, an angel speaks, "If anyone worships the beast and its image and receives a mark on his forehead or on his hand, he also will drink the wine of God's wrath, poured full strength into the *cup* of his anger" (Rev. 14:9–10 ESV, emphasis added).

Jesus knew the Scriptures and was fully aware of this imagery when He prayed in Gethsemane with the cross looming so very near: "My Father, if it be possible, let *this cup* pass from me; nevertheless, not as I will, but as you will" (Matt. 26:39 ESV, emphasis added).

We know what unfolds. We know that the Father did not let the cup pass from Jesus but required that He drink it to the full on our behalf. We know that the disciples were going to drink a cup too—a cup of suffering (Matt. 20:23). But Jesus' cup of suffering was different from theirs—and from ours—because Jesus' suffering was under God's anger. Jesus drank the cup of God's wrath, a cup that had accumulated the fury of God against all evil, every act of adultery, disobedience, murder, hatred, rage, offense, betrayal . . . all of it over all time.

This is the cup Jesus drank on the cross.

There was another cup offered to Jesus at the top of the hill at Golgotha. As He was suffering, the merciful centurion handed Him a cup. Jesus sniffed the liquid. It was wine mixed with myrrh, a mild narcotic to dull the pain. But Jesus knew He was not meant to dull the pain nor numb it in any way. He was to feel it. So He refused to drink the elixir. No denial. No numbing. He endured being fully awake to the pain so it might produce all its intended work.

Because Jesus drank from the cup of suffering and wrath, that cup became the cup of salvation. The cup of suffering became the cup of joy. Turns out, it's the same cup.

Hebrews 12 says that it was for the joy that was set before Him that Jesus endured His tortuous death on the cross. But to get to the joy, He first had to be willing to drink the cup of suffering. In the midst of His excruciating pain, Jesus fixed His gaze on His Dad and held on to the joy that He knew was coming to Him on the other side of the cross. He showed us that we, too, can have joy in the midst of our suffering because of the joy that is set before us—and no one can take it away from us.

> "So you have sorrow now, but I will see you again; then you will rejoice, and no one can rob you of that joy." (John 16:22 NLT)

No one and nothing can take away our future joy at the grand reunion that is going to take place when Christ returns and all things are made new (Rev. 21:5). Endless life, eternally satisfying and delightful, is headed our way. Jesus led the way with His death and resurrection, and that joyful new life is promised to us as well. But remember, friends, to get to the resurrection, we have to pass through the crucifixion.

We will suffer, but we will never suffer as Jesus did— ever—because Jesus drank the cup of wrath for all the sins of all mankind. Though we will suffer, it will always be under a canopy of grace and love, never wrath and judgment.

This is the cup that Jesus invites us to partake of as He did. It is no mythic holy grail that we must search for in order to find eternal youth and infinite joy. This cup is real. We drink of it to remember Him when we celebrate the Last Supper, proclaiming His death and resurrection until we see Him again. We drink of it to proclaim as they do in the Episcopal mass, "The blood of Christ, the cup of salvation."[5] We take up the cup to join in the fellowship of Jesus and all the saints who precede us with a hope that is untouchable. We take up the cup of blessing, and as we do, we sing as David did, "I will lift up the cup of salvation and call on the name of the LORD" (Ps. 116:13). And, finally, we drink of the cup because we would not shun any of that which Christ deems necessary to shape us into His image.

We can rejoice over that.

Rejoice

What makes a sinner rejoice?

When his sins have been forgiven.

What makes an angel rejoice? In Luke 15:10, Jesus tells us, "In the same way, I tell you, there is rejoicing in the presence of the angels of God over one sinner who repents."

What makes God rejoice? When we come trembling before Him, giving our whole hearts to Him in committed love.

What makes Jesus rejoice? Let's look at Luke.

The seventy-two returned with joy and said, "Lord, even the demons submit to us in your name."

He replied, "I saw Satan fall like lightning from heaven. I have given you authority to trample on snakes and scorpions and to overcome all the power of the enemy; nothing will harm you. However, do not rejoice that the spirits submit to you, but rejoice that your names are written in heaven."

At that time Jesus, *full of joy* through the Holy Spirit, said, "I praise you, Father, Lord of heaven and earth, because you have hidden these things from the wise and learned, and revealed them to little children. Yes, Father, for this is what you were pleased to do." (Luke 10:17–21, emphasis added)

The scriptures say that Jesus rejoiced greatly. Another translation is that Jesus was exuberant (Luke 10:21 THE

MESSAGE). He was exultant! Why? Because He passed His authority on to us. He shares His victory with us. We get to do the same work that He does. We get to share in the joy of our Master (Matt. 25:21 ESV).

What makes you rejoice?

Is it knowing the incredible sacrifice of Jesus, His willingness to drink the cup of God's wrath so that you will never have to? Is it His death on your behalf? Is it the fact that your sins have been forgiven? Oh yes.

We can have joy, because we can know God's strength in our weakness. Because God's mercies are new every morning. Because as we walk through this valley of this shadow of death, we are never abandoned or alone. Our God goes before us, and He is behind us, around us, and within us.

We can have joy, no matter what sorrow or suffering we are currently enduring, because we have been chosen by the Father and He will never turn His face away. We are loved. Forever. And nothing can ever separate us from that love.

We can have joy because we are engraved on our Father's heart and on Jesus' nail-scarred hands, and in Christ we are victorious. The suffering doesn't have the final say. In fact, God is going to use it for even more good to come into our lives.

James 1:2–4 tells us to "consider it pure joy, my brothers and sisters, whenever you face trials of many kinds, because you know that the testing of your faith produces perseverance. Let perseverance finish its work so that you may be mature and complete, not lacking anything."

God is growing us up. He is committed to making us the mature bride of Christ:

> And not only this, but we also exult in our tribulations, knowing that tribulation brings about perseverance; and perseverance, proven character; and proven character, hope; and hope does not disappoint, because the love of God has been poured out within our hearts through the Holy Spirit who was given to us. (Rom. 5:3–5 NASB)

The sorrow and grief that come are real, and we have a God who is well acquainted with them. He doesn't ask us to ignore our grief but to invite Him into it that we might bear it together.

No matter what, we can know an internal defiant joy because death has been defeated. Life has won. There is suffering, yes. But always there is the potential for joy.

In the face of the ultimate reality won for us by Jesus, we don't have to pretend that life is better than it is, that we don't hurt as much as we do, or that we feel happy when we are not. We are invited to be fully alive, awake, alert, and oriented to the truth, and to know that because of Jesus, we can be defiantly joyful.

Father, I trust You but You know this is hard. I'm hurting, God, and I need You. Would you please come for me in this place? I don't understand why this is happening—yet here and now, I proclaim that You are good and that I trust You. I need Your strength, Your mercy, Your comfort, and Your help. I pray for the grace to endure and I pray that You would bring Your life and Your kingdom here. Shine Your light into this situation and bring Your healing and deliverance. Please, bring me more of Your presence, God. I am looking to You. I love You. I ask You to intervene. Fight for me, Jesus. Thank You that You have not abandoned me. Thank You that You love me. Thank You that You have good plans for me and that You are stronger than anything and everything I face. You alone are God. You are mine and I am Yours. So come, Jesus. Come. And use this to help me know You, love You, and be transformed by You even more deeply. In Jesus' name, I pray. Amen.

Three

Whiplash

I lift up my eyes to the hills. From whence
does my help come? My help comes from
the Lord, *who made heaven and earth.*

—Psalm 121:1–2 RSV

The weather changes dramatically in Colorado, sometimes from one hour to the next. Yesterday it was seventy degrees, so I sat on the front porch for a bit in the afternoon, my body drinking in the sunshine with the gulps of the long deprived. The sun shone brightly, soaking into my parched skin. Soon, though, it became too hot for me to stay outside. This morning, however, snow covers the ground. It is a still and frozen world. Yesterday's canvas has been painted over with white, recreated with endless possibilities by an artist wishing to try again. A forty-degree temperature change is not such an unusual thing here, but I wonder if the dramatic shift in the nature of the world feels like whiplash to the birds who are no longer singing.

I am suffering whiplash of a different sort. It has a physical effect, but the source is emotional. My whiplash is delivered when I run up against my manic failure.

Just yesterday, when I awoke, I felt on top of the world.

I've been doing so well. I ate healthy yesterday. Yay, me! There is hope! Look, see! With God all things are *possible! I can do this with Him.*

Then, later in the afternoon, when I was exhausted and dangerously alone on a last-minute grocery-store run, my efforts to stay "on plan" were destroyed by a self-sabotaging sniper donut. I know. I kept track. I wrote it down. Okay, it was two donuts.

I'd woken up with hope yesterday morning, but this morning I'm waking to hope deferred, laced with shame, and my heart is crashing. I am on the other end of the spectrum, thinking completely different thoughts.

I am exhausted. I feel so overwhelmed. What was I thinking? I can't do this. I don't want to get out of bed. Maybe I won't. Let's see how long I can last in here.

My struggle with weight triggers so many things that threaten to steal my joy. It's a strange thing to feel your body getting larger. When it first started happening, I could ignore it. *Weight fluctuates regularly, right? My clothes still fit, so it's not a big deal.* Granted, they were perhaps a little tighter, but, hey, they had just come out of the wash. Denial is a powerful thing.

Denial cannot last long, however. It smacks up hard against reality. When I noticed a roll and an expanding stomach where there wasn't one before, it caught me off guard. *What?* I was genuinely surprised. Somewhere in the pain and grief of last summer, I had opened Pandora's box and released all the well-worn paths of years of addiction. Those roads delve deep in my brain and my patterns of coping. Like a dam breaking, I felt swept away by my own inability to stand against the current. The dry, firm ground of health that I had chosen up till then crumbled under my hungry heart. Old habits returned with a wicked vehemence. My weight slowly crept up, and so did the self-contempt—that inner dialogue of berating my weakness and lack of strength to turn to God in my hardest moments. I felt like a hypocrite.

This morning, I feel like one once again. I believe God is good. I believe I *can* do all things through Him who strengthens me. I even believe I can do this—this getting Pandora back in her baking-section box and living committed to making healthy choices based on love.

But then, I'm not out of bed yet.

I turn my heart to pondering, *What does it mean to be defiantly joyful in this moment when I am dwelling on the ancient path of shame and disappointment in myself?* Those paths are made of quicksand.

I need a Savior.

I have one.

My friend Lisa Beck says that God planned our rescue before we even knew we were in trouble.

I'm in trouble. I know it now. And the temptation is to hate myself for it. Do you know this place sometimes? Did you get irritated with your spouse this morning over some silly thing and speak to them with a stinging contempt no one deserves? Did you buy that alluring thing when you had pledged to stay within your budget? Did you indulge in pride when you compared yourself to a struggling friend who had always seemed so smug? Did you become angry at God and blame Him with a veiled rage because your life is not turning out the way you ache for it to? How do you handle your heart in this place?

Sometimes I feel as though I am sinking into a swamp of self-judgment. Self-judgment can feel to me, well, justified. But that hard kernel of shame does not yield a fruit of self-control or change or repentance or any other good thing in my life. Instead it turns into a shield that affects my capacity to receive love. It becomes the foggy, warped lens through which I view my every relationship and myself. I simply don't believe I am loved or lovable. How could it possibly be true?

In fact, left alone, the little hard kernel of self-judgment grows like an aggressive cancer, wreaking havoc in my life. The small stone becomes a massive rock that is too large for me to move. But God—still two of my favorite words—*but God* is in the business of moving stones. There is no ancient, grave-sealing, love-blocking weight that He cannot overcome.

And I have a part to play. So do you. The core of my heart needs to align with the truth that judging myself harshly is neither my right nor even remotely godly. God has asked me to renounce self-judgment, so, as valid as it feels, I am obeying. Renouncing judgment breaks the painful claim of hatred I've imposed upon myself and allows love to come in. It allows grace to come in—both for me and for others. Rather than becoming prickly and defensive, I give up my position as judge and hand it over to the One who is the rightful Judge, Jesus Christ. If He can forgive me and love me, well then, who am I to withhold love and forgiveness?

I must choose again in this moment to surrender to God. I have to choose to believe Him and all the incredibly marvelous things He says about me and feels toward me. And with that, my heart rises. The chains of self-contempt are shattered by His never-changing grace and give way to the holy chords of singing repentance. Conviction takes the place of condemnation, and I walk into the joy of the prodigal being embraced by the Father. He has not turned His face away. He has been waiting, waiting and watching with keen eyes that have beckoned my return all along. I choose to return and raise the gaze of my soul to His ever-kind face. He has not been judging me. He has been wooing me out of my sin.

I know there are times when I am blowing it. But "Judged" is not the banner over my life. "Loved" is.

That same banner is blowing in the wind over your life as well. And no wind of change, no temperature drop, no frozen landscape, no whiplash of failure, and no Pandora's box of self-contempt can change that.

Now and always,

> May our Lord Jesus Christ himself and God our Father, who loved us and by his grace gave us eternal encouragement and good hope, encourage your hearts and strengthen you in every good deed and word. (2 Thess. 2:16–17)

Whiplash Strikes Again

It's getting close to the new year as I write now. It's as good a time as ever to look back, take stock, sit with Jesus, and ask where He'd like me to grow, to focus, or to challenge myself in this next season of my life. It's good for us all to do that. On a regular basis. My desires for this past year were deep: to grow in knowing the heart of my Father as I never have known it before and to become stronger. In every way.

Here's the encouraging thing: I believe those desires flowed straight from His heart. I still do. That's the thing about asking Him what He wants for you and asking what it is that you really desire. The two meet. And knowing it's His desire as well as your own provides the fuel to press on when the exuberance of beginnings wears off.

This past year, God has been coming for me. He's answered my prayer to know Him as Father more deeply than I could have imagined, and my journey of wonder and amazement continues. Physically I've been on the mission to reclaim lost ground in my strength and health. And I have been getting stronger. Measurably.

One of the joys of becoming more physically fit has been sharing the experience with my husband. Working out together. Running together has become our new normal, and we love it.

Well, we did love it until I couldn't do it anymore. I hurt my lower back. I hurt it badly, which affected my piriformis (the little butt muscle under the glute), which pressed against the sciatic nerve and stopped me in my tracks. Whiplash yet again from strength to weakness.

It's been pain and hobbling and the inability to lift my leg an inch off the floor for a long time, and the prognosis is, at best, that I'm halfway to recovery. Maybe two more months. Maybe four. Or so I thought. I've since learned that it wasn't a lower-back issue or even a muscle injury at all; it is severe osteoarthritis and my hip is beyond repair. A hip replacement surgery is in my near future, and then the slow process of regaining strength will begin.

I've been thwarted. Again.

It happens.

It's a bummer.

I'm not complaining. Okay, yes, I am, but come on! It hurts!

One thing this situation has done is make me more aware of all the people around me who are shuffling or using canes or needing the mechanical cart at the grocery store. It makes me think of and pray for all those I know and those I don't who live with constant pain. It makes me remember the years I suffered with deep depression and lived under a heavy cloak of despair, slogging my way through to life. It makes me wonder how I pressed on through that and how marvelously God has come for me. It also makes me realize that I have grown insensitive to the masses of humanity surrounding me who are hurting and suffering daily.

I'm not sure how I forgot.

My injury might have struck with the force of whiplash, but the eye-opening perspective that came with it has been a gift. Even with this incredible gift, though, I still find myself struggling to get my heart on firm ground with God. My occasional battles with discouragement have, well, discouraged me. Though I've experienced a fresh overflowing of mercy toward others during my time of injury, I've noticed that I haven't extended it to myself. How is it that I can be gentle with others but berate myself so harshly when I'm alone?

My husband once found me lying on the floor, crying over the pain and my failure to live well in it and adamantly, forcefully even, caught my heart declaring that my interpretation of things, my self-accusation, was untrue. It has been such a back-and-forth internal battle. My husband says I'm handling it amazingly well. But inside I don't feel that way. I'm aware of my impatience. My irritation. I feel as though I'm not handling it well at all and that I'm a weakling. I tell myself that I should never be overcome emotionally and certainly not spiritually by pain.

Anybody relate?

I'm so grateful that earlier in the year God came for me and revealed His overwhelming, all-encompassing, always-been-there-and-not-going-anywhere love for me—for all of us—in new and life-changing ways, for it buoyed me in the midst of my injury. I did not question His goodness or His love for me. But then, the very day I said that out loud turned out to be the very first day I did.

Dang it.

I felt thwarted. Did He thwart me? I don't think so. Injuries happen in this world. I met a woman who was suffering from a piriformis injury. She had hurt herself while transferring laundry from the washing machine to the dryer. Sheesh. You never know when your life might change.

I don't believe God caused my injury or hers, but man oh man, is He using it. I'm being stretched into the uncomfortable but oh-so-necessary realm of receiving. I like believing that I am capable. I don't like not being able to stand for long enough periods of time to make dinner or clean up after it or shop in the grocery store or put away the laundry. Even walking to the mailbox is out of my realm for the moment. This is especially hard for me because, like many people, I hate asking for help. But I need to. It's so very humbling, *and* it's teaching me. How's that for whiplash?

At one time or another—no, many times—we all experience situations as I have that come with the force of whiplash. We *all* do. And then what? It's the "then what?" that matters.

My hope for this next new year is that these things surfacing in my heart, things that aren't very pretty, would be like dross bubbling to the surface for removal. My prayer is that I would be more deeply cleansed. That God would use it to make me more like the woman we both want me to be. That it would change me in good, softening, and holy ways. That I would get better. And not forget.

Being suddenly hit with an injury is a physical whiplash that strikes with a manifold effect. But in it, let me be softened and let God's glory be increased. And let the healing come.

And if it hurries up, well then, so much the better. In the meantime . . . mercy.

It Happens to Everyone

Whiplash goes around. Like a car rear-ending you when you are merely sitting at a stoplight waiting patiently for it to change, it strikes you when you least expect it. We are a vulnerable race, human beings. Even the stronger ones are vulnerable.

In my marriage, my husband is the strong one. Okay, yes, I'm a strong woman and all that, but I am also graced with a husband I am able to lean on for even more strength. Among other things, he can open a jar of pickles when I have given up. He can hang up the heavy planter high on a chain. He can effectively use the snake thingy to free a deplorably clogged toilet. He can pray with power and he can drive a tractor and he can arrange flowers. He is my very own Renaissance man, humble and kind and strong. And then he was thrown by a horse with more power than he had, and his physical strength was put on a very long hiatus.

"Would you please get me some apple juice?" my husband, John, asked one morning after the accident. He was standing in front of the open refrigerator, longing for juice but unable to get it for himself. One wrist was in a cast, the other in bandages recovering from surgery. He helplessly held both hands out in front of him.

John is a capable man, as I mentioned, and he is used to being leaned on. This needing-help thing was both new and uncomfortable for him. And it lasted for months. It was hard—for him. For me, it was an opportunity to love and care for him. I am not by nature a patient woman—and I will confess that when he asked me for apple juice my heart rose up in irritation—but, extraordinarily, for most of John's recovery, I loved having him need me.

He needed me! Clearly. Unapologetically. Indisputably. Externally and internally. The man needed me. He couldn't tie his own shoes, let alone get down a jug of apple juice.

What John learned in those months is partly detailed in his book *Walking with God*.[1] What I learned is that I came alive when I was needed. John's dependence was a great gift to me and also, in the end, to him.

We are honed both in our needing and in our being needed. Whether we are the ones experiencing whiplash or the ones walking beside those dealing with the aftereffects, there is joy and growth to be found in the giving and receiving of loving support.

Yesterday I washed my twenty-one-year-old son's hair in the sink. He had been living his life fully and unencumbered when he dislocated his shoulder in such a painful and unique way that it required surgery to repair. He's recovering from surgery now and is unable to move or lift his arm for the next six weeks. His whiplash, too, was from independent to dependent. From being strong to being weak. He can't drive. He can't tie his shoes. He can't yet wash his own hair. Call me crazy, but I was thrilled to do it. I hobbled over to the kitchen sink with a pleasure I felt I should hide. It's not that I was glad that he couldn't do it himself. It's just that I was, well, a *little* glad he couldn't do it himself. He needed me.

I still remember leaning over the kitchen sink as a child and having my mother wash my hair. Every time I have the pleasure of going to the hair salon these days, I remember the way my mother's fingernails once also gently worked the lather into my scalp. In those childhood moments, I felt cared for. Loved. Safe. Did she love doing it for me as much as I loved washing my own child's hair?

We value independence. Mobility. Self-sufficiency. Yay.

But we are a dependent people. Dependent on air, food, water. Needful of others. Needful of God. He is our divine helper, our *ezer*, without whom we will not be able to live a life of meaning filled with what matters most. Truth. Beauty. Goodness. Love.

How do we get our thirst quenched when we are unable to quench it ourselves? How do we care for ourselves when we are unable to move? How do our needs get addressed when they are too deep for us to tend?

We need God. Realizing that we need Him is a profound, humbling, and extraordinary gift—the first step toward a wholeness of soul. Because when we turn to Him, we find Him. When we call out to Him, He answers. When we cry, He comforts—not merely or even primarily in the tangible and immediate way we may yearn for, but more often in a deep, steadying encounter that becomes clear only as the moment has passed. We are not alone. We are not orphans left to figure out life by ourselves. We are dependent on our God who is *with us*. Do you think that maybe God loves it when we realize this? Don't you love it when someone you love needs you? I believe God enjoys it when we call out to Him, recognize that we need Him, and lean into His unending, grace-filled strength.

These days my son needs me in ways that are tangible, and his need of me is a gift to this mother's heart. My availability to him is my gift to him. With my own injury, I also need others' help in ways I couldn't previously have imagined. At our house, it is the weak caring for the weak. And I am learning that being needed is a gift. My own weakness is providing an opportunity for others to rise and shine on my behalf, offering their strength with glad hearts, or perhaps sometimes irritated ones. It's been a whiplash from what I wrongly believed would bring me life to what actually does.

Recognizing that we are all needful of one another and of our good God is the breeding ground for mercy. That's how it works in the kingdom of God. Win-win. Gift-gift.

An Abrupt Turn

"St. Patrick's Breastplate," a powerful prayer attributed to Saint Patrick of Ireland, begins in this way:

> I arise today
> Through a mighty strength, the invocation of the
> Trinity,
> Through belief in the Threeness,
> Through confession of the Oneness
> of the Creator of creation.[2]

"I arise today through a mighty strength." Oh, wouldn't that be nice to say every morning? I want that to be true of me, but what is true for so many of us on too many mornings is "I arise today through a fog of forgetfulness." We have to claw our way out of the cloying depths of unbelief back into the dawning light of truth and breath.

Different mornings provide alternative options of discouragement. Thoughts that frequently take our hearts captive upon arising include:

> It's going to be a bad day.
> I don't want to get up.
> You are a failure as a mother, father, friend . . .
> You do not love well.
> You are alone.
> You are on the outside.
> You are a selfish person.
> This is all too hard.

And repeat.

Do you know what yours are?

This morning, I arose through a veil of guilt and accusation. Today's litany coming against me was a shorter version. The accuser was battering my heart with *Failure. Failure. Failure.*

The crushing weight of shame was reinforced by memories (cruelly twisted but seemingly real interpretations) of my failings, evidence parading across my mind that I was not being a good friend, wife, or mother.

But the prayer continues:

> I arise today
> Through the strength of Christ's birth with His
>   baptism,

Through the strength of His crucifixion with His
burial,
Through the strength of His resurrection with His
ascension,
Through the strength of His descent for the
judgment of doom.[3]

Wow. Well, okay then. We don't arise through our strength to figure it out or to pull it off or to change or to become an amazing person who loves everyone at all times perfectly. We certainly don't arise today by arguing ourselves and the oppressor of our souls out of accusation.

We arise today and every day by turning our gaze onto Jesus and what He has accomplished for us—because we needed Him to accomplish it.

We don't arise today by our strength but *by His*.

We simply don't have the capacity to get out of bed in the morning when we're buried under a landslide of accusation and shame, the evidence of our faults piled high, ready to convict us and send us into a prison of self-loathing.

No.

While still feeling the weight of failure this morning, I turned my gaze onto my Jesus and His finished work on my behalf. I began to ask Jesus for the truth and to tell it to myself: *I am not a perfect friend, but I am a good one. I fail as a wife and mother, but I am not a failure.*

I took my gaze off my performance and turned it onto the

King and *His* character: His faithfulness. His goodness. His mercy. His strength. His might.

> I arise today, through
> God's strength to pilot me,
> God's might to uphold me,
> God's wisdom to guide me,
> God's eye to look before me,
> God's ear to hear me,
> God's word to speak for me,
> God's hand to guard me,
> God's shield to protect me,
> God's host to save me
> From snares of devils,
> From temptation of vices,
> From everyone who shall wish me ill,
> afar and near.[4]

I hide myself in Him, and in Him I find my strength to rise. For He does not accuse us; He blesses us. He invites us all further up and further in to be changed into His likeness, and not to gaze at our weaknesses or fears but to gaze at Him. Perfection. Might. Our Victor. Our Savior.

> Christ with me,
> Christ before me,
> Christ behind me,

Christ in me,
Christ beneath me,
Christ above me,
Christ on my right,
Christ on my left,
Christ when I lie down,
Christ when I sit down,
Christ when I arise,
Christ in the heart of every man who thinks of me,
Christ in the mouth of everyone who speaks of me,
Christ in every eye that sees me,
Christ in every ear that hears me.[5]

This morning, like so many days in my clay-footed life, I need mercy. My Father offers it to me. Jesus has won it for me. The Holy Spirit beckons me to receive it. I need mercy, and I know it. In that knowing comes a great gift. I turn my heart again to my kind and understanding God and confess to Him that I need mercy. His answer swamps my heart with a too-good-to-be-true reality that leads to a crumbling of hopelessness and shame. My self-loathing collapses into His love. My self-condemnation melts into His arms that welcome and soothe. I have blown it. The blowing now has become the wind of the Holy Spirit. *Ruah* is here. His breath shepherds my heart into my Father's, and there mercy triumphs over judgment. I may stay in bed a bit longer, but now it is not out of despair. Now I cozily snuggle into His forgiveness, His love, His heartbeat of hope.

The turning of my heart from lies to truth can happen as quickly as whiplash. It is the good kind, the kind that brings life. Sometimes I am not strong enough to orchestrate it, but our God is stronger. Always. And for that I am defiantly joyful. He invites us all to make the turn, and when we look to Him, He gives us the power to do it. We can have hope, no matter if we wake to accusation or to celebration, because our God is with us.

Four

Interference

You make known to me the path of life; you
will fill me with joy in your presence, with
eternal pleasures at your right hand.
—PSALM 16:11

I recently ran out of two of the three medications and herbal supplements I regularly take for emotional health and thought, for some reason, I could manage without them. To refill them takes phone calls and a long drive, after all. And how come they didn't just come with the automatic refill in the mail like they're supposed to? *Oh well. I'm fine. It's not worth the effort to refill them,* I thought. Which could easily be translated to *I'm not worth the effort to refill them.* I was doing so well when I let this slip. I wasn't considering the fact that part of the reason I was doing so well was *because* I was regularly taking my medications. But after a few weeks, I wasn't doing fine.

Daydreams of quitting my job and moving to an unknown town began to surface. Family gatherings began to feel really stressful and hard. I broke down in tears when a simple phone call dropped after I had been on hold for ten minutes. I started having to hide in my bedroom when dinner conversations got too lively. Call me Miss Self-Aware (or not), because it took a few weeks for me to realize that the weight I was struggling under wasn't due to a fissure in my character; it was a reaction to my decision to suddenly stop taking medications that I needed.

I thought I could easily press on without them. Surprise! I cannot. Not yet anyway. Jesus had to intervene on my behalf with a merciful reminder that I had to tend to my needs. Once I realized this and got all I needed refilled, I hoped I could get back to my normal self within a week. Everyone around me hoped so too.

When my brain chemistry is not functioning as it is meant to, holding on to the reality that joy is my birthright becomes hard. It can feel audacious, ridiculous even, to grip firmly onto our right to defiant joy when we are living under an emotional or physical struggle or come up hard against a painful reality of life.

I was with a woman recently whose husband had left her

the week before. She had a disability that had progressed to the point that she was now completely confined to a wheelchair. She was totally dependent on others' care, and her husband had been overcome by the pressure. Their marriage was a submarine with unseen fractures, and the pain had brought them far down into deep waters. The small cracks had expanded, the fault lines were exposed, and the relationship had exploded. He moved out.

This woman's body had been racked by pain for a long time, her heart for even longer. Her marriage had shattered into pieces many years before her husband called it quits. They had become mean to each other. Cruel even. And they had been for almost a decade.

Her physical pain coupled with the pain in her soul was so deep that the only possible relief she could imagine was to die. But she had three elementary school–age children. Because of them, she was still choosing to cling to life, even if that clinging felt tenuous. She knew that her children would be in unbearable sorrow and confusion if she abandoned them, and also they would be left to their father, whom she no longer trusted. When we met, she was in so much despair that the best possible answer she could think of was to take her children's lives right before taking her own. Hearing this whispered confession broke my heart completely, but with today's epidemic of suicides sweeping across the country, thoughts like these are a dark reality more common than we realize.[1]

The wonderful truth we *can* cling to, though, is that

darkness does not have to have the final word. This is where defiant joy comes in. Joy is light. Joy is conceived in faith and gives birth to hope, not to despair. It could not be more opposite to death and darkness.

This woman's story is an extreme one—one that called for the intervention of Jesus, as well as people trained to help her overcome such dire pain. And her story is not over yet. Far from it. She may not have had hope, but I have it for her. Not because I know her to be a resilient woman, but because I know a God for whom nothing is impossible (Luke 18:27). He can turn ashes into beauty. He can transform despair into hope-filled praise. He can call the dead and decaying places in us into fruitful life. It is what He loves to do.

He can reach her. He can reach me. He can reach you. He is the God who intervenes. He is the God who interrupts. He is the God who interferes. He interfered with me through an emotional crash. He is interfering with her through a crucible of desperate proportions. We need Him to interfere with all of us through every and any means available to Him.

I love the story of a certain man whom Jesus interfered with, much to his initial chagrin. Remember when Jesus met the man possessed with many demons in Luke 8?

So they arrived in the region of the Gerasenes, across the lake from Galilee. As Jesus was climbing out of the boat, a man who was possessed by demons came out to meet him. For a long time he had been homeless and naked, living in the tombs outside the town. As soon as he saw Jesus, he shrieked and fell down in front of him. Then he screamed, "Why are you interfering with me, Jesus, Son of the Most High God?" (vv. 26–28 NLT)

The man in this true story was tormented by demons to the point that it was impossible for him to live a healthy life. He was isolated from his family and friends, not able to work or do anything other than endure the excruciating torment. And after many years of this, Jesus showed up. When He did, the man came running naked to Him (that must have been a little unnerving—at least for the disciples), shouting, "What are You doing here? Why are You interfering with me? This is my life. I'm fine. Leave me alone!"

Huh. We all know he wasn't fine. His life had not been his own for quite some time. In fact, it wasn't him at all who was shouting at Jesus to go away but the inner tormenting demons compelled by fear. And Jesus, mighty Love incarnate, refused to leave. Instead He interfered; He intervened.

Jesus crossed the Sea of Galilee, all sixty-four square miles, to get to this one man. And He has crossed galaxies and heavenly realms to get to you. He passed through unimaginable opposition and endured unfathomable suffering to get to you. To mess with you. He has come, and He is coming still. To save us. To heal us. To help us. To love us. To guide and comfort us. And to interfere with our lives—particularly in the places we do not want Him to.

Yes, it can be uncomfortable, but remember who Jesus is. He has the right to interfere.

Jesus asks us to look at things. He asks us to reengage with people and passions in the places that we have been hurt or have given up. He asks us to let some things go. He asks us to pick some things up. He asks us to repent. He asks us to obey. He messes with our style of relating. He messes with our choices of books and movies and even the jokes we make.

He interferes with us in the places we have hidden, in the places of safety and soothing. And He calls us out.

He's been interfering with me.

Has He been interfering with you?

The man possessed by many demons asked Jesus, "Why are You interfering with me?" You know the answer. It's the same one He has for you. Because He loved him. And He loves you.

If we are to find healing and true joy, we need to lean into His interference. And to do that, we must first ask ourselves the question, what part of our lives is He interfering with? Think about it. Picture Jesus approaching you with searching eyes that look straight into your soul, and ask Him, "Where are You interfering? Where am I resisting?"

If you're struggling with finding the answers to these questions, try thinking about it this way: Where do you ache? Where do you hurt? Where do you feel conflicted? What are you longing for? What have you been called to that has felt thwarted? Where have you felt diminished?

It's important that we recognize and name what we have been living with—and under. That we hold our lives before God and ask for His revelation of where we need a deep and true repentance. Perhaps the place where fear has taken hold. Or shame. Shame over the way we feel or how we're living, or shame over our past mistakes and our present ones. Whatever it is inside our hearts that needs a work of God, Jesus has come and is coming even now to get to that part of you. He's coming for the places you have tried, for a multitude of reasons, to bury. He is coming to prompt you into knowing that your true identity and your value as a person come from your position in His heart as His beloved child. And He is interfering with your life so that you will live it more fully with and in Him. But first we must let Him in.

Interfering for Our Healing

We had been planning this vacation to the garden isle of Kauai for four years. My family and I had been anticipating it for so long, and now it was finally happening. It was time to begin packing. Then, the day before we left, John and I got in a doozy of a fight. *Hoo boy*. Sadly it wasn't a mutual throw-down argument. That would have been easier to deal with. No. It was a hard conversation my husband needed to have with me, shared with deep pain.

I had hurt John, and I had been hurting him in ways I was blind to for a very long time. It all came to a head over a puppy I had wanted to buy. All right, over a puppy I had already bought without talking it over with him. I thought he was going to be happy about it. I was oh so very wrong. In pursuing what I wanted and what I thought would bring life to our family, I ignored what he wanted. My insensitivity in this situation revealed a pattern in my style of relating that had been doing damage to his heart for years. The timing of this revelation could not have been worse.

The romantic long walks on the beaches of Hawaii that I had imagined became solitary walks of tears. I saw what hurt I had caused John in my thoughtless action, but more importantly I saw the pain I had caused him over the course of our entire marriage. Days of repenting—what Dan Allender calls "an internal shift in our perceived source of life"[2]—followed, as did many uncomfortable conversations with my husband. God revealed ways that I had been arranging to "save" my own life, and I realized the cost of that maneuvering was losing the life I truly wanted: a life lived for love. The vacation I had been imagining for so many years turned into a heart surgery by a skillful God.

Sometimes it is God who thwarts us and our plans to pursue what we think we need. God sure thwarted me this time. He interfered with my plans to escape into an Eden-like tropical world and enjoy days of ease. But the fruit of His interference brought deeper healing and intimacy to our marriage than I could have hoped for. I thought I needed rest; Jesus knew I needed an intervention.

God interferes with us a lot. He interferes with our inner diatribes; He interferes with our style of relating; He blocks the paths we wrongly think will lead to life. He interferes to bring us up short so that we might see where we are taking the wrong turn. He wants us to truly know Him and enjoy Him. He wants us to live lives that will lead us more deeply into His wonderful heart.

Oftentimes God's interference feels painful, but we need to see the mercy and compassion in our Father's eyes. We need to breathe and consider the possibility that God understands, that He's not holding a whip to make us run faster or a ledger to keep track of our sins. No, He is holding out His arms to gather us in and invite us into deeper repentance and life. He interferes because He loves us, and He wants us to know who we are as people and who we are *to* Him. And that's where the healing begins.

Here is the truth we must remember in the middle of this sometimes painful healing process: we matter to the heart of God. He hasn't taken His eyes off us. He thinks of us constantly. He has hopes and dreams for us. God planned on us before He made the stars, and He planned on us being His. He planned on us sharing our lives with Him on this wild adventure. And His plans are good. Just like all the disciples of the Lord Jesus Christ who have gone before us and who surround us now, we are uniquely and wonderfully made, and the world needs us.

Ephesians 2:10 reminds us, "For we are God's handiwork,

created in Christ Jesus to do good works, which God prepared in advance for us to do."

Sometimes this is hard to believe. Sometimes the pain of that healing process makes us wonder if we even have a role to play. *Is it too late? Have I missed it? Blown it? Am I disqualified? Do I really have anything of value to offer?*

What is behind that question? What's underneath it that mocks us when we are feeling lost? It is fear that maybe we don't have anything to offer. This is something people have struggled with long before our time. Let's go back to Luke:

> When the herdsmen saw it, they fled to the nearby town and the surrounding countryside, spreading the news as they ran. People rushed out to see what had happened. A crowd soon gathered around Jesus, and they saw the man who had been freed from the demons. He was sitting at Jesus' feet, fully clothed and perfectly sane, and they were all afraid. Then those who had seen what happened told the others how the demon-possessed man had been healed. And all the people in the region of the Gerasenes *begged Jesus to go away and leave them alone, for a great wave of fear swept over them.* (Luke 8:34–37 NLT, emphasis added)

You might expect that the people would have rejoiced at this great miracle of healing, but instead they were overcome by fear. Much like we are at times. What would Jesus like to say to us about our own fear? Where does God's interference with our plans and desires make us want to tell Him to "Go away!"?

When I became a Christian, I was zealous for God. "I will go wherever you want me to go" was my heart's cry. People I knew were going to Africa on missions, and I thought that was where God would call me to go too. Someplace far away at least. Someplace ripe with the possibility of heroic faith. I was willing to go. I wasn't afraid of going. What I *was* afraid of doing was staying.

But God called me to stay. He interrupted my own plans and asked me to engage with Him in ministry right where I was, and I wasn't happy about it. I feared that my life would lack significance and meaning. I wanted fireworks, but He held the matches.

It turns out, Jesus' interference with my desire to be an international missionary was an invitation for me to humbly surrender to Him. It became an opportunity to trust Him with my future. The fruit of that decision was being released from the burdensome pressure of making my life unfold in a way that was completely my responsibility. I had been carrying that weight for a long time. When I let it go, something in my heart began to rest in new ways. Jesus restored an important aspect of our relationship to me.

Perhaps the best thing we can know is that when Jesus interferes with our lives, it is because He wants to restore us.

That's what Jesus came to do, by the way: restore. Remember when He had His first public moment in the synagogue after His showdown with Satan in the desert? He was handed the scroll of Isaiah. Jesus unrolled to the passage Isaiah 61:1–2, and as He read aloud He proclaimed the purpose of His coming:

> "The Spirit of the Lord is on me, because he has anointed me to proclaim good news to the poor. He has sent me to proclaim freedom for the prisoners and recovery of sight for the blind, to set the oppressed free, to proclaim the year of the Lord's favor." (Luke 4:18–19)

Jesus came for our deepest good—so that we might be able to live with a whole heart that is capable of receiving the love of God and of loving Him in response.

In order to get us there, Jesus often has to interfere with our lives so that we may come to know His love. To believe He adores us. To believe it is our hearts that matter to Him more than our behavior. Our hearts affect our behavior, of course, but God desires our love more than our duty. He voices His complaint against the Israelites in Isaiah 29:13 when He makes His charge:

> "These people come near to me with their mouth
> and honor me with their lips,
> but their hearts are far from me."

Clearly God wants our hearts. He is after our love. He wants us to choose Him in the face of the brokenness of the world and our own lives. He wants us to believe He is still for us even in those times when He steps in our way and blocks the trajectory of our lives.

Honestly, when He interferes with me, my initial response is not gratitude but frustration. *Why are you bothering me now? I'm busy with my life. I don't have time to stop.* But something deeper in me knows I need this; I need to make room for Him when He nudges His way into a place where He was heretofore not welcome.

It's humbling to be interfered with. It was humbling when the day before our vacation my husband said with a heaviness of heart that he needed to talk with me, that, for the good of our marriage, I needed to understand how my behavior was hurting his heart. I was able to receive the interference because I knew it was born out of love.

That's the key: love. We have to remember that the *reason* God interferes with us directly—or through situations or relationships—is the same reason He interfered with the man possessed by demons. He interferes because He loves us. Because of this, we can posture our hearts to receive His gentle instruction. We can rest in knowing that our God is not an angry Father bent on our obedience but a loving Father working for our wholeness.

Jesus will get in our way because He *is* the Way. He wants to heal and restore us. He will interfere with us because He needs us to know that first and last we are our Father's beloved children. He wants us to know who we are and to step into all that it means.

Let Jesus interfere with your life so that you may be

transformed by His love, by His magnificent, immeasurable, uncontainable, enticing, powerful, stands-in-your-way, ridiculously joyful, all-consuming love. And then? Then you, too, will have a story of hope and joy to share with others; you, too, will be able to proclaim the great things that God has done.

Five

Greener Grass

He makes me lie down in green pastures.
—PSALM 23:2

The tree was moving. There was no wind, but the leaves were fluttering with life. It was as if it had been quickened by an invisible command that no one could hear. No one, that is, but those who could fly.

I approached the tree to get a closer look, and as I did the leaves erupted with the sound of hundreds of beating wings. As one, the tiny birds took to the air and swept the sky like a banner of silk waving in the breeze. I had come too near. Watching this aerial symphony take flight filled me with joy, their fluttering beauty a surprise of delight. They did not go far. A nearby tree had suddenly become much more appealing, and the flock settled there, setting it ablaze with tiny movements.

As the saying goes, the grass was greener across the street.

And now a cow was bellowing. I heard the cry go up and recognized the call of a mother separated from her child. It was a cross between longing and irritation. "Where did you go? I told you to stay right here." Dinner was ready, her udder was full, and her little one was nowhere to be found.

Without looking, I knew where the calf would be. It would be grazing just on the other side of the fence. The grass is always so much greener there.

For me growing up, the grass was greener at my grandparents' house. My parents didn't fight there. I wasn't as invisible at their home as I was at my own. Oftentimes, when we arrived, my grandmother had a present for me. Why didn't we live there, for heaven's sake?

When I was four years old, I determined that we *should* live there. Well, at least I thought that *I* should. We lived in Kansas City at the time, while my grandparents lived in New Jersey, and my young heart decided that I would walk there. I hadn't been off my street before, but I figured that if I walked a good twenty minutes, I would get there. In fact, I drew a map. I packed my little red-and-white case for dolls and took off.

I made it two blocks.

Later my family moved to Southern California, and I was

no longer interested in running away to my grandparents' home. The allure was gone. Instead I wanted to go back to our neighborhood in Kansas City. The green grass was now growing there. My mother was happier there. My sisters and brother weren't angry and sad there. When we lived there, my father raged much less. In Kansas there were thunderstorms and the fragrance of fields and friends who liked me, and it was my *home*. It was in Kansas that I had felt God begin to woo me to His heart. Now my life was unknown and frightening, and I felt so alone. Where was God in this place?

I decided the only answer was for me to run away back to Kansas. I got on my bike to ride to the airport so I could catch a plane back to my real home. I got many blocks farther this time, but then, with tears streaming down my face, I realized I didn't know how to get to the airport, let alone come up with a ticket. I had to turn back.

What about you? Have you ever gone looking for a reprieve—a taste of beauty, a respite, an escape—when your world became too complicated or too overwhelming? Did you think everything might be generally better somewhere else, anywhere else? Maybe you were a little girl who went to the swing set or the tree fort. Maybe you went to your grandmother's house or walked in a field. As a young woman, did you try to run somewhere that felt safer when life became too threatening? Where did you go? To a book? To a movie? To a man? To church?

Were you a little boy who, searching for greener grass, escaped into the wild of the backyard or the Amazonian ditch behind your home? As a young man, did you go to magazines, to music, to sports, to books, or to women, not knowing you were searching for a way to soothe your soul? Or maybe you did know.

The world does become too complicated, too overwhelming, too filled with pain so much of the time. As children, we don't have the capacity to make sense of it, let alone process it. If our lives become too filled with trauma, a part of us disappears. We push down what we can't understand or resolve and instead go looking for greener grass to distract us from the ache. But that doesn't really work. At least not in the long-term.

We need to stop our running. We need to tend our hearts. One of the best ways we can do that is by honoring the story of our lives, by letting that part of us and our past that has been tamped down rise back to the surface, and then inviting Jesus into it. If we are to find our way to an authentic life characterized by joy, one that isn't constantly looking for something better elsewhere, we will need to face the truth about our lives with merciful honesty and choose to linger in it long enough for the Holy Spirit to do His gentle yet persistent redemptive work.

I haven't always walked in this kind of Spirit-filled honesty myself. For a long time, I didn't know I needed to own my story—really own it and not run from the reality of it and, in my own way, tell it—in order to facilitate healing of the very real damage done to my soul. Because of my embarrassment and fear, as well as a lack of understanding of how healing works, when I told the story of my life in the past, I left the most impactful parts on the editing-room floor. I am only now beginning to skim the surface of telling my full story. I recently told it in more depth to a small group of trusted people in a covenant of confidentiality. But even then I could not tell all. I cannot tell all now. But I can tell more. And I can tell you that what I've found on the other side of all that redemptive telling is an open door to healing. The more honest we are able to be about our lives, the more healing and life we will know.[1]

And healing, while it can be a longer process than we'd hoped, is a grace-filled one that always brings joy.

Mint-Green Grass

Years ago, when my three sons were young, I would take them to the park near our home to swing and climb and play whenever it was sunny outside. I remember one day in particular. As I sat on the bench near the playground, a shiny new green minivan pulled up to the park. At the time, we were a one-car family. We felt blessed simply to have a car that ran, but, well, it wasn't a very nice-looking car. It was an older, dinged-up four-door sedan, and I confess that I really wanted a minivan. Badly. So as I watched this green minivan approach, I wondered, *What would my life be like if I drove a car like that?* That cool green minivan in mint condition was the greener grass I longed to reach.

I figured that if I drove *that* car, everything would be much, much better! If I had *that* car, my house would be neat and tidy. My furniture would match. My laundry would be put away. I would be a woman who planned meals out two weeks in advance. If I drove a car like *that*, then our bills would be organized, our checkbook balanced, and our spice rack alphabetized. I would never feel sorrow well up in my heart in the dead of night. I wouldn't feel haunted by failure. I'd have the Bible memorized! There would be world peace! No one would go hungry! Oh, wait. I was getting carried away. This was a *car*, mind you.

Then the lovely, fit woman got out of the pretty minivan with her healthy, happy children who were wearing clean and matching clothes and confirmed my every suspicion. Green minivan equals a good life. Further, being lovely and fit plus having children who appear happy and healthy and who wear clothes with name brands also equals a good life. Which, as you well know, translated very quickly in my heart to, *My life is a bad one. It is without deep value or worth.*

Theodore Roosevelt is thought to have said, "Comparison is the thief of joy," and boy, was he right. We tend to compare our worst to another person's best, and we come out poorly. We compare another person's smile with our inward sadness, and we hide in shame. We compare our body to another person's fitter one, and our joy shrinks. We compare what we imagine another person's life to be like with our known reality, and we grieve. We compare ourselves with others, and our hope melts, our sense of value dissipating like the mist.

Comparison is a problem.

It is easy to believe that someone else's life is better than our own and that if we only had "fill in the blank" we would be happy. Judging another's green field of a life from the view of our dusty brown patch is tempting, but comparison is a faulty lens. Letting our imaginations run away with us through unhealthy and untrustworthy comparisons steals our joy rather than increasing it.

We may choose to "jump the fence" of our lives through myriad means, but ultimately we will return and find our hurting and unsatisfied places are still waiting for us to tend them. But here's the good news: oftentimes that longing deep inside our hearts for something better is an invitation from God to bring further healing in those hurting and unsatisfied places. It is our lives' own grass that God wants us to be able to enjoy as green, and to get there we must spend some time taking care of it. Until we do, our hearts will continue to clamor for soothing. We need to learn—I need to learn—that the clamoring isn't the problem. It is, in fact, the calling card of grace.

Running To, Not From

The day my family gets together every year to decorate our Christmas tree is a beloved ritual, a night of cheer. It's the welcoming of the season, one filled with the family traditions of enjoying the first Christmas cookies of Advent and listening to the same songs on the stereo that have played for more than two decades. Things aren't quite right on this night until Miss Piggy sings. This particular year, though, things felt off. My children were all gathered. The tried-and-true cookies were there. And all I wanted to do was sit on the couch. I occasionally roused myself to enter into the festivities and put on an ornament or two, but very early on I started thinking there were enough decorations on the tree already and *good grief, who has this many ornaments? Next year, we should get a smaller tree.*

Normally I love this ritual. I even love that three-quarters of the way through, the boys are going to disappear downstairs to play video games and leave John and me to finish up. So, as I sat on the couch with these thoughts, wishing things were different than they were, I knew something was wrong internally. I felt exhausted. It took such effort to engage, let alone add a red ball or enjoy the festivities. Where did my love of this tradition go? Why was I discontent with the situation? What was going on?

God drops things in our laps at just the right time. He puts barriers in our paths that look like roadblocks but are really gifts in disguise, beckoning us to take a closer look at what's going on inside of us. We can either step over them or choose to pick them up and examine them for the potential they may hold. Failure is ripe with goodness. The longing to run away or escape our lives for any greener grass is the opportunity to seek God in the midst of it, to learn something deeper about both us and Him. Exhaustion and sadness often hold the door open for a more restful and joyful life.

If we will let it, the door opens to remind us of the person we wanted to be but have left behind in the chaos and disappointments of life. When the sadness refuses to be silenced and the feelings arise that this is not the life we had signed up for, we can either go to shame or to God. Is it a sin to want to be happy? Is it wrong to want to know an inner restfulness that is not subject to the whims and torrents of a life that refuses to slow down? I don't think so. God does not think so either. We are made for bliss. We are made for inner peace. If it were not so, why would all humanity throughout history seek it with such a driven and often frenetic passion?

I need a refuge. I need rest. Sometimes I feel the overwhelming need to simply escape from the clamoring within and without, and, occasionally not knowing what to do with this feeling, I run away to a movie. Sitting in the dark and eating popcorn provide a little respite. I have a momentary flash of happiness when the opening credits and trademark soundtrack begin to roll. There's the woman holding a torch! There's the world turning with an engulfing light! Yay! But then, after a couple of hours, I come out of the movie, and all that I left in the car still awaits me. Too often this temporary-escape thing doesn't work out the way I'd hoped.

Not that I am opposed to temporary escapes. Look at my life, and you will know that. It's just that sometimes the motive behind them isn't a search for joy or laughter or a shared experience. Rather, it is born out of a refusal. Too often I run away from my own heart out of a refusal to engage it. It takes energy and space to become present to the truth of my inner world, and when I am overwhelmed, the thought of such activity is, well, overwhelming.

It's overwhelming, anyway, until it can no longer be ignored because God places a roadblock in my path that forces me to face the fact that I am in need of a Savior. I get to the place where I am pressed to accept my own weakness, and it causes me to hold my life and heart open before the merciful eyes of a loving Father. It draws me up short to see where I fall short in my own strivings so that I may once again discover the source of my identity, which is found right where I am, smack-dab in the middle of God's loving gaze.

God calls us to run away to Him, not from Him. He asks us to not fix our gaze on other people's lives and compare them to our own but to look to Him for the source of our worthy life. He asks us to find our rest in Him. *He* is our resting place. When I am exhausted, the temptation is to turn from God, thinking that He requires more from me than I have to give. I may believe I need to muster some passion from a dry well and focus on improving my performance. I may think I need to pull myself up by my bootstraps when I'm too tired to put my shoes on. I am wrong.

We are called to be honest and to bring God our authentic selves. He asks us to come before Him in the state we find ourselves in. Look at David. The Psalms are filled with his passion. He comes before God when he is desperate and when he is rejoicing, when he is overcome and distraught, and when he is exultant and victorious. We are meant to do the same.

In every moment, God does not ask us to share life with Him as anyone other than the person we are. We are not meant to be anyone else. We are to come to Him with child-like trust that He will not turn His face away. He invites us to tend our hearts in His loving gaze. His arms are open wide. He is the greener grass in which we will find solace, soothing, refuge, and joy.

As we choose to draw near to Him, to rest in the safety of His gaze, the redemptive work of God gains ground. Joy begins to bubble up, and the kingdom of God advances in our lives, inevitably spilling over onto others' lives as well.

Open your heart to it: to Him, to life, to vitality, to the power of God moving within and through you. Ask God to grow your capacity for joy. He can do it.

He is a good Father who knows how to give good gifts. Remember in Matthew 7:9–11 when Jesus asks, "Which of you, if your son asks for bread, will give him a stone? Or if he asks for a fish, will give him a snake? If you, then, though you are evil, know how to give good gifts to your children, how much more will your Father in heaven give good gifts to those who ask him!"

Ask away. Ask in faith, knowing that He is the Father we all wish we had.

A Good Father

I grew up with an earthly father who did not know how to show his love for me well. I witnessed friends' fathers being tender with them, even calling them special names like "Princess." My father didn't call me anything, rarely even acknowledged my existence. Looking back—and he's been gone for more than thirty years—I can now see when he tried to show his love for me, when that was his intention. Sometimes. Perhaps he didn't know how. Perhaps he didn't have the capacity, but, regardless, there were those times when I did see his love, even if I struggled to feel it.

I was arrested for drunk driving when I was eighteen. Escaping from the pain of my life, I turned to drugs and alcohol at an early age. In excess. My father was out of town when I was arrested, and when he returned I was charged with informing him about my stint in jail and my upcoming trial. When I said I had something to tell him, he guessed, "You were arrested for drunk driving." I was fundamentally surprised that he had been aware of the life I was living. Maybe he'd cared more than I realized.

Later, when I went to court, my father sat right beside me in his best suit. I felt his support. I felt his care. I didn't sit in the courtroom alone. He didn't condemn me; he already saw my remorse. Though I had to bear the weight of the consequences of my actions, I didn't bear them without his strong presence right beside me that day.

Perhaps you have memories of your earthly dad fighting

on your behalf. Perhaps you only know what you were meant to have by not having it at all. Either way, each of us possesses an innate knowledge that we are meant to be fathered. And that comes to its fullness in the One who calls Himself our Abba, our Daddy, who bears our burdens alongside us, whose heart dreamed of us and beat for us before we were even twinkles in our earthly parents' eyes.

You *have* a good, good father. He *is* Father. It's not merely what He does; it's who He is. You don't have to pack your bags and run away, searching for a better one. You already have the best one. Your Father is the One who has been pursuing you, protecting you, and loving you your entire life.

God, your Father, is love. He loved you as a child, and He loves you now. Right now. But you have questions about that, don't you?

I was with two sisters who were raped by their stepfather, and they will still tell you that God is love, that He is a God who heals, and that it is well with their souls. When they first said that to me, I was speechless. I believed them, and I also knew I was in the presence of the miraculous. Trusting in God can be difficult in and of itself, but trusting in God as a loving Father in the context of such betrayal from an earthly father figure? That is far from easy. Every time I hear a story like this, I want to ask, "But how? How do we continue to trust and love our God when He has let such harm befall us? How do we believe He is our good, good Father?"

That is *the* question.

We live in a fallen world. Untold atrocities happen every

moment. They happen to people we love, and they happen to you and me. But we look at the cross and the love of the Father poured out for us through the blood of His Son, and the question is forever answered. Mysteries abound. Questions are okay. But the answer remains unchanged.

My friends are loved. I am loved. You are loved. All this time, the things you have been longing for that spoke to you through books, nature, swing sets, tree forts, and every imaginable form of beauty was Him. It was your Father calling you home to His heart, the only safe place for yours.

This is the deepest truth, and the world and all its sorrow and harm cannot touch it.

Remember what Paul told us in his letter to the Romans:

For I am convinced that neither death, nor life, nor angels, nor principalities, nor things present, nor things to come, nor powers, nor height, nor depth, nor any other created thing, will be able to separate us from the love of God, which is in Christ Jesus our Lord. (Rom. 8:38–39 NASB)

We live in a larger story. This is not the land of the white picket fences with a chicken in every pot. We don't live in Oz or the Kansas of its wizard. There is an incredibly good ending to our story, but it often isn't on this side of eternity. Joy comes. Here. Joy is available. Now. It is birthed in the unchanging love of our Father. To know God's love is to be able to stand in gusts and gales, and though our bodies be knocked over, our souls remain standing strong. We need His eyes on our stories, and we need to see our stories in light of His.

It's as C. S. Lewis wrote: "I believe in Christianity as I believe that the Sun has risen, not only because I see it, but because by it I see everything else."[2]

The larger story, the gospel, reminds us that we live in a fallen world and sin abounds. We know that we have an enemy and he is loose, roaming the earth, searching for those he can devour, shred, and maul. He works through fallen people, even through broken, imperfect Christians, to steal, kill, and destroy. And God loves those people. The Father loves them (and us) so much that He sent His Son to die for all of us. He is for you. He fights for you. He woos you. He protects you from further unimaginable harm that you will never endure, and even in the worst of pain, He is fierce on your behalf.

You can rest in His love. The end of your story is a good one. The grass we will walk on one day when Jesus returns is lush and thick and fragrant.

Do you need Him to redeem the word *father* for you? He can.

Do you need Him to redeem your story for you? He will. It's why Jesus came.

Do you want to know Him as Father? He wants that too.

You are loved. Right now. When God looks at you, He sees the one for whom He gave everything and won everything so that you could be with Him forever. You are chosen. You are the apple of His eye. You are the joy that was set before Jesus. Ask God to help you know that. Ask for His view on your life.

Ann Voskamp wrote:

> Because God's writing your story and He never leaves you alone in your story, and His perfect love absorbs all your fear and His perfect grace carries all your burdens, and your story is a happily ever after because Christ *bought* your happily ever after so you *always* know how this story ends: *You're going to be okay.*[3]

Ask God to help you see your life as He does. Ask Him to reveal Himself as Father to you. Ask Him to enlarge your capacity for joy. Because when He does, the only running you will do is straight into His arms.

Six

A Divine Exchange

To bestow on them a crown of beauty instead of
ashes, the oil of joy instead of mourning, and a
garment of praise instead of a spirit of despair.
—ISAIAH 61:3

My birthday is today. For me, birthdays are a mixed bag. I have had amazing birthdays when I have been celebrated well by friends and loved ones, and I have had birthdays with no celebration at all. One birthday, in fact, was so bad that it not only did *not* go well but it resulted in a deep rift in a cherished relationship. But there have also been many years when I have come out of my bedroom in the morning to find that John has decorated the living room with streamers and balloons. One year he was out of town and I came out expecting nothing, but my young sons surprised me by having gotten up early and done the decorating themselves. How kind! How wonderful! How splendid! Even though it may feel a bit awkward in the moment, deep down I love being celebrated.

This year, though, I honestly couldn't care less. It's been a rough year. It's been particularly rough these past few months, and I am weary. Soul weary. Tears come whenever I have a spare moment to allow them to flow. Losses and betrayals that my family and I have endured have brought me to my knees. I'm currently walking through the last days of a very dear and close friend's life, bearing my own sorrow while helping to shepherd the hearts of those around me who love him and are losing him as well. It is a holy season and a hard one. I don't have the energy to blow out candles. I don't have the vim and verve to drum up an exuberant response to any "Happy Birthday" phone messages I may be blessed to receive. Did I mention that I'm tired?

I am aware that I have a choice to make this very morning. I have been given my life as a gift from my God, and today is a marker of the many years I have been blessed to live. I need to honor that gift and the people who wish to celebrate it with me. I need to choose to have my heart rise in thankfulness. It may be difficult, but it is my choice to do it, and it is the right one to make. I'm not going to fake a buoyancy that I do not possess. But I am going to turn my gaze away from sorrow to joy, from resentment to thankfulness. In other words, by the grace of God and the strength of Christ who lives within me, I am going to choose love.

We are, each one of us, invited to make a divine exchange. We are called to trade looking at our circumstances for looking at our victorious God, and by doing so we give the root of our being the nourishment it needs to thrive.

There won't be streamers and balloons today. My husband is weary as well, as he walks alongside me in this extremely tough season. But we will choose to set our eyes on Jesus, and there will be joy.

Mourning for Dancing

Ecclesiastes 3 says that "there is a time for everything, and a season for every activity under the heavens . . . a time to weep and a time to laugh, a time to mourn and a time to dance" (vv. 1, 4). Yes, there are times when we need to weep and mourn, but eventually God calls us to exchange those times for laughing and dancing. I've seen this on full display in the life of Craig, a joyful and wise man—a sage, really—who works in our office.

One day early last year, Craig went into the staff kitchen and suddenly, all alone, began to dance. There was no music playing. He was not wearing earbuds or listening to a song. He was listening to his own internal drummer. He simply, in the quiet, began to dance. Julie, whose office is positioned in such a way that she can see directly into our kitchen without even craning her neck, noticed this and grew curious. She walked over to him and asked him what he was doing. His response? "Julie, I have learned that when you feel like dancing, you just have to dance."

This is a man known for his wisdom, his gentleness, his deep faith, and particularly his joy. Joy in the midst of battling cancer. He makes jokes that warm the heart right in the middle of a dire diagnosis. He is a man who says, "I have many reasons to grieve, but I have many more to worship."

That is a heart set on Jesus. The deepest reality of all our lives at every given moment is that we always have a reason to worship. We always have a cause to be joyful. And sometimes that manifests in dancing.

Second Samuel 6:14 tells us of the time that the ark was brought into Jerusalem and, with exuberant joy and to mixed reviews, David danced before the Lord with all his might. His dancing flowed from a heart bursting with worship and gratitude. It's as Craig says: when you feel like dancing, you've just got to dance.

Dancing as a joyful response to God in worship is a wild and beautiful thing. It is the outward expression of a heart that cannot contain its joy and, in that experience, explodes like yeasted bread overflowing its borders.

Do you think God dances? How could He not when you consider that He created rhythm and music and bodies that respond to it with toe tapping? A friend of mine says that dancing is how God gets from one place to another.

Hebrews 12:29 says our God is a consuming fire. Have

you ever sat mesmerized, watching a fire move? It's as if it's alive. Licking. Rising. Flickering. It is active. It dances. It is a visual representation of what Becky Allender describes as "the wild dance of the kingdom":

> In Greek, *perichoresis* means "rotation or dance," and in early church theology it became a way to talk about the interplay of the members of the Trinity. The Trinity dances together in a holy mutual indwelling without loss of identity. I love to imagine each person of the Trinity—the Father, the Son, and the Holy Spirit—voluntarily circling the other two and dancing with joy and love for one another.[1]

In Matthew 11:17, Jesus bemoaned the people's lack of faith, saying, "'We played the flute for you, and you did not dance; we sang a dirge, and you did not mourn'" (NASB). Jesus was saying that dancing would have been the better response, the better choice to make.

When was the last time you danced?

There is a time to refrain from sorrow. But always it is a time to fix our gaze on Jesus. And when we do, we make the divine exchange, trading mourning for worship.

Death for Life

Life has a way of wearing on a person. Under the weight of losses, pressures, failures, and endless demands, something in our souls begins to wither. Passions dry up. The zeal of a beginning turns into a despairing end. A stone falls heavily down, crushing our will, and in those very places where Jesus once gave birth to vibrant hope, we yield to the grave. Our hearts retreat with a "no more" as death gets ahold of us. But the cemetery is not where we are meant to live.

I had the privilege of visiting Israel a few years ago. It was an incredible experience to go to places I had read of and wondered at for so long. One day, I was awed to be standing outside of Lazarus's tomb. While there, the pastor leading our little group asked us to inquire of God if there were places within us that we had closed in a grave. I knew the answer for me was yes. I was tired. I was hurting. Betrayal from a friend had left me wanting to shrink back from all people. My passion for life had dimmed. My zeal to tell others of the wonders of Jesus had faded. I realized a part of my heart had become buried. And then I felt His call.

Jesus' call to us is the same as His call to Lazarus as He stood before his grave in John 11: "Come out!" he commanded. "Come alive!" We are not meant to live in a tomb. Our callings are needed in the world; they are not to be buried under the burden of others' demands or judgments. Pain comes, but it does not get to seal our graves.

So I ask you, where is death for you? What song has died on your lips at the critics' continual shaming of your voice? Jesus commands you loudly and firmly to "come out." And He says it with tears. He is fierce in His instruction and in His intercession for you. He has life for you. Life. Ask Jesus where the tomb holds you and then answer His call.

You are needed. And your help is needed to remove the graveclothes that too many around you are continuing to wear. Make the exchange that Jesus won for you from death to life. Trade the lie for the truth. Replace the stone pinning down your heart with wings that will strengthen you to soar. Ask Jesus to help you do that. He would love to. It's what He came for.

Addiction for Freedom

Addiction is a hard beast to kill. After spending so many years in the company of various versions of it, both my own and others', I'm beginning to believe it cannot be killed, only tamed. Or exchanged. Yes, the best way to handle an addiction is to exchange it. Just turn it in.

Early on in my Christian life, I exchanged an addiction to drugs and alcohol for the high bestowed by carbohydrates. Actually, the stranglehold of drugs was one I was released from, rescued from, delivered from solely by the intervention of Jesus. I could not have gotten myself free from that addiction any more than I could have sprouted wings. I was saved.

I was saved, but I was not completely healed. I didn't truly know the battle involved, the strength required, or the diligence needed to tame the allure of addiction until I got entangled with the enticement of food's quick fix. Bingeing has a numbing effect. A shot of sugar (my go-to) brings with it a quick calm. I can purchase a release of dopamine in my brain at any grocery store. Whenever I am in a panicked place, my sinister friends of baked sweetness soothe and comfort for a little while. But only for a little while. Then the siren song of need calls me again to "come away with me, my beloved." I am caught in a net. My body no longer registers being full. Hunger is not sated. Desire rages, and in its cold demand I often exchange truth for a lie. I bow at the altar of a false god. I have an affair with a false lover. I cannot free myself from its clutches, though I have tried. And tried. And tried. And tried. And I am tired. But I remember what Gabriel proclaimed to Mary: "Nothing will be impossible with God" (Luke 1:37 NASB).

I'm currently a part of a program that is not a diet but a "lifestyle change." We've all come to know that's what is required, right? I can't do an eating plan for three months and then afterward go back to the old ways of eating and expect the loss to last. Expecting the results to change when the behavior doesn't? That's crazy! I should know. Been there. Done that.

I'm all over this lifestyle change. I believe in it. Like a drowning woman clutching to a life raft, I'm clinging to the hope that it will come to my rescue. But will this actually save me? What fruit have I seen coming out of this change? "You will know them by their fruits," remember? (Matt. 7:20 NASB). The truth is, it is too easy to make the wrong exchange on this quest for rescue. In the battle of the bulge, the wrong fruit still ripens when the high is not sought out in carbohydrates but in a fit body. The highest goal in that exchange remains relief. Food may not be the drug of choice, but exercise has taken its place. Or portion control. Or rigorous self-constraint, living within the boundaries of a toned chain-link fence. The obsession does not end; it merely transfers. And it remains centered on the self.

That is not freedom.

I'm not after such an earthly exchange. I'm after a divine one.

Jesus came to bring it. He alone can address the craving in my heart. To partner with Him in this, I must learn to feast on His abundant goodness and the hope of His ridiculous joy. I must believe, every single day, that Jesus Christ is my life, my hope, and my freedom. I need to camp my thoughts and my heart in the truth laid before me of all He won for me at His death, resurrection, and ascension.

I am growing in doing so. Some days, taking my thoughts captive is like training an obedient dog. Other times it feels like a wrestling match with a tiger. But I am learning, ever so slowly, that it is possible. This fixing-your-gaze-on-Jesus thing can be hard work, but it's hard work that bears a soaring freedom.

Fear for Love

As I get older, the seasons seem to pass more quickly. As I write this, winter has passed. The mountains have exchanged their winter stoles for colorful sundresses. And summer in Colorado is a marvelous thing.

Even now, butterflies, delicate flowers with wings, are fluttering by. Thousands of starlings wing their way as one shifting geometrical masterpiece. As Wendell Berry wrote in *The Art of the Commonplace*, "Outdoors we are confronted everywhere with wonders; we see that the miraculous is not extraordinary but the common mode of existence. It is our daily bread."[2]

It's good to get outside. And the people of Colorado do it en masse. Come summer, gyms empty and outdoor activities, always rampant, explode. Hiking. Climbing. Running. Biking. Racing. Swimming. If it's outdoors, they're doing it, and my family is in the thick of them. Or, rather, my husband and children are in the thick of them. For many years, my not-fit and not-slim body have prevented me from joining them. But that's only partly true. What has really kept me from participating is fear.

And now my family wants me to go down the Colorado River in an inflatable single-person kayak with them and navigate the rapids with joy. Do I stay or do I go?

In years past, I would have been afraid the rental company wouldn't have the required life vest to fit me. I'd be afraid that I might not fit in the kayak. I'd be afraid that I'd hit a rock and go under, but much more terrified that someone in my family would. I'd even be afraid that I'd have to go to the bathroom halfway down and there would be no place to stop. I'd be afraid of being too afraid to ask them to stop!

Who thinks this stuff is fun?

Fear is a familiar companion to many of us, but it tries to hide its true nature and stay in the shadows of our souls. "I'm not here. This is just realism, practicality, wisdom," it lies. But fear is not our ally, not our friend, and definitely not our helper. It causes us to be untrusting. Still, for most of us, it runs deep. It came to us through wounds and pain, and because of it we shrink back.

But Hebrews 10:39 tells us, "We do not belong to those who shrink back." At least we are not meant to.

Fear causes us to make agreements like, "I cannot *trust* you will stay, so I will do everything in my power to *make* you stay." Or "I cannot trust that I will not be hurt, so I will keep my distance from everyone." Or "I cannot trust that you will not be hurt, so I will do my best to keep you as safe as possible in every conceivable way."

Yet God wants us to trust. To trust *Him*. God is nothing if not trustworthy: He is good. He is faithful. He is for us. Everything He has done has been out of love for us. We can see this even in the extravagance of the world He created and placed us in.

Look around. Look at the beauty and the splendor of creation. Look at the majesty presented in the sunrise, in the sunset, and in the stars; the sky is strewn with abundant glory. Look even at the Colorado River flowing with endless whimsy, wonder, and strength. And look at yourself. You are fearfully and wonderfully made, a vessel of the Holy Spirit, the very dwelling place of God, because

He loves you and wants to share your life with you every single moment.

God is our partner. He is our ally. He is our friend. He is our helper. We can trust Him. And because we can trust Him, we no longer have to live in fear. We can step out in trust, in faith, and live with His strength.

Where is He inviting you to trust Him? With your family? With your lack of one? With an adventure, a move, a class, a friendship, a kayak trip? Where is He asking you to step out in faith and go forward not in your own strength but His? In your own healing? In pursuing more of His life for you, in you?

No matter what area of your life God is calling you to trust Him with, know that because of His trustworthiness, you don't have to be afraid. You can pray, "Jesus, come and uproot my fear. Replace it with a revelation of Your goodness. Overwhelm my fear with Your love. Come into the gap in my soul between what I profess to believe and what I truly do. I want to know You. Deeply. Truly. In the way that lends itself to easily trusting You. Come for me again, oh Faithful Friend."

So, for me, stepping out in trust looks like me agreeing to go float the rapids in an inflatable kayak with my family. I will pray for our safety and wisdom and God's protection. And I will do it with joy. I hope to have my eyes open and my heart aware and attentive, on the lookout for God's gifts of beauty and love that He is always, always, *always* generously scattering around us to draw our hearts to His.

I will do this and much harder soul-searching things

because our God is good and I can trust Him. Because He is beckoning, and I do not want to shrink back. Because my life is a gift, and I want to live it. Because He loves me, and I don't have to be afraid. Because God is my strength, and in Him I am strong as well.

As always, be it a birthday or a birthright, the right exchange is needed. Sorrow for joy. Fear for freedom. Silence for song. Melancholy for celebration. Shrinking back for pressing through. My weakness for His strength. Distrust for faith. My bent for His way. Daily I must choose to make a divine exchange of death for life. Though I may have many reasons to grieve, I always have many more reasons to worship. Because of Jesus, my feet may feel heavy, but my spirit can dance.

> For the LORD will deliver Jacob
> and redeem them from the hand of those
> stronger than they.
> They will come and shout for joy on the heights of Zion;
> They will rejoice in the bounty of the LORD—
> the grain, the new wine and the olive oil,
> the young of the flocks and herds.
> They will be like a well-watered garden,
> and they will sorrow no more.
> Then young women will dance and be glad,
> young men and old as well.
> I will turn their mourning into gladness;
> I will give them comfort and joy instead of sorrow.
> (Jer. 31:11–13)

Seven

Expectant

*Though you have not seen him, you love
him; and even though you do not see him
now, you believe in him and are filled
with an inexpressible and glorious joy.*
—1 Peter 1:8-9

Nothing can be done without hope.
—Helen Keller

We have a little cabin in eastern Colorado right smack-dab in the middle of nowhere. It's rustic. It's small. It's in cattle country, empty land but for endless sage. It's an hour's drive to the nearest grocery store. And it's quiet. Well, kind of.

We are surrounded by cattle ranches, and every now and then the cows break the silence and make their presence known. Still, the bucolic sound is comforting. It comes mixed with the buzzing of flies and the whirring of hummingbird wings. Then there's the creaking of the old cabin's metal roof. It groans as it expands under the warmth of the sun. It stretches itself out to welcome the heat, and when the warmth fades and the coolness of evening sets in, it will groan again, creaking back into itself like an old woman folding her achy bones into a rocking chair. It, too, is a comforting sound.

Now comes the whisper of the wind in the aspens. Like water flowing over stones, the breeze shakes the heart-shaped leaves and winds its way down the valley. The cries of a family of hawks join the symphony. There is a pair that nests on the hill behind us every year, and they now have three little ones to teach how to hunt. To watch them soar is to watch a company of ballerinas take to the sky.

But that is all. The intermittent notes of nature's song. Birds. Bees. Bugs. Cows. Wind. And the panting of my hot and happy dogs. Background noises you barely notice, save when immersed in the quietude of nature. The sounds of silence indeed.

This quiet stillness of the natural world is hard-won. You must travel far to get to it. It is a silence deep enough to allow me to hear the drumming of my blood through my ears and the rising of the questions from my soul. Silence is a luxury, and one that I long for, yet I rebel a little against it with my own inner engine, blocking the sound of the questions of my heart. My hope rises that in the quieting of life's surrounding din, I may at last begin to hear the voice of Love.

"Be still," God says. "Be quiet. It is in the silence that I am most clearly heard, and I have much to say to your restless, weary heart."

Wait

The hummingbirds are fighting over the feeder. One in particular is being a bully, stabbing at his competitors with his fierce sword of a beak. There's plenty for everyone, but this ruby wonder will tolerate none other than himself to drink from what he has claimed. Still the others will not give up. There are five vying for a spot at the feeder, and there is only space for four. Another hummingbird watches and waits from a nearby hanging basket. Does it know that in its waiting for just a few moments it will not only save itself the thrust of a sword but also get its fill of sugar water?

It can be hard to wait.

More often than not, I am too much like the frantic hummingbirds at the feeder, determined to get my fill and fighting for my place at the table. If I don't elbow my way in and make something happen for myself, I risk going without. If I want something good to happen, then I am the one who must make sure it does. I am the one responsible for my own life, am I not?

Well, yes. And no. I have a role to play, yes. But there is

no way that I can pull off my life. I can't arrange for all the goodness I want to come my way. The good news is, God already has. Goodness and joy await us. We are promised in Psalm 23:6 that "surely goodness and mercy shall follow me all the days of my life" (KJV).

We but need to have the eyes to see it. As long as we are looking down, we won't see the clouds above us. As long as we are focusing on our clay feet, we won't see our new hearts. As long as our hearts are heavy with doubt, we will miss the wonder that surrounds us. The joy that is meant to be ours could elude us. It all depends on where we gaze. When we look at Jesus, we receive the courage to believe and the ability to wait.

Expectant of Good

This has been my year to know physical pain as I have never known it before. I have known limitations and anguish, disappointment and at times despair.

It has been going on for one very long year made up of long months, longer days, and sometimes excruciating moments. But I must add here, it has been going on for *only* a year. And though it does change my physical capacities in the future, I know the pain will not last forever. I must turn my eyes once again to the Author with expectancy.

God is the Author of all things good. Including joy. He says we can have joy in the midst of everything life is throwing at us. He says we can have peace in the midst of every season and storm that come our way. And they will come our way. In John 16:33 Jesus says, "In this world you will have suffering." Yes. We know that. But He continues with hope: "But take heart, I have overcome the world."[1] Suffering does not have the final word. Every source of pain has been defeated by the victory He has won for us.

Still. The truth remains that suffering comes. And sometimes it comes with a vengeance.

My neighbor suffers from lupus. She has had it for a very long time. Symptoms flare up beyond her control, making it impossible for her to live her life as she would like to. She loves to garden; she often can't. She loves to entertain, but it is frequently outside her capacity. She wants to care for her ailing parents, yet too many days she is unable to leave her home or even get out of bed. She falls and bruises easily and often is covered in hues of blue. She gets sick, and the illness becomes complicated and long. She is well acquainted with pain. But in those times when she can move, when she has the strength to sit outside, she calls me over with a smile and a tone of voice filled with warmth and joy. "Hi! I haven't seen you for a while. What's going on with you?"

Another friend has cerebral palsy. She is accident-prone; she falls and things break. She has broken both her legs, her wrist, her collarbone, and three ribs on four different occasions just this year. We talk on the phone via Skype, and she is frequently in bed. Or in a hospital. And often in these many months, in a wheelchair. Sometimes she gets discouraged. Sometimes she gets angry. But she doesn't stay there. Her heart turns to hope and to healing. Her heart turns to her God and to caring for others. I am in awe. When asked, she will describe the litany of appointments, the coming surgeries, the lack of physical mobility, and the frustration of not yet being able to begin physical therapy. But then she will ask, "How are you doing?" and sincerely want to know, freely engaging other topics with laughter that is ready and deep.

Who are these people? What is it they have learned that I so desperately need to? How can they wait for wellness with such undimmed perseverance?

James, the brother of Jesus, wrote, "Count it all joy . . . when you meet trials of various kinds" (James 1:2 ESV). Like my two friends, James knew suffering. He lived in a world without antibiotics or immunizations or running water. He lived in a world of crucifixions and tyranny and severe persecution. And yet he said to count it all joy, even in the face of our broken world filled with depravity, sin, selfishness, hatred, and horror.

How did James and my two friends walk in such illogical joy and remain pregnant with hope? Let's look at what James went on to say: "For you know that the testing of your faith produces steadfastness. And let steadfastness have its full effect, that you may be perfect and complete, lacking in nothing" (James 1:3–4 ESV). Times of testing can also be times of refining and growth. The counterintuitive truth is that suffering can deepen our hope. It enlarges our hearts so that we can know the love and presence of Jesus in ways that we would not if we did not go through the stretching process.

In my friends' cases, they've learned to lift their eyes above their prescription bottles. They hope for relief and pray for it, believing in a God who heals, and they wait in the quiet, being stretched in the process. They wait, knowing that healing is coming. They wait, growing to know Jesus much more deeply, in a way I long to.

These gals are just two examples of women I walk with whose lives are filled with physical suffering. And through my own injury, I have had my eyes opened to pain in a way I never would have chosen. Yet in it God is teaching me things I need to learn, and it seems that once again His chosen method is suffering.

Who is this God who is so determined that we know His presence that He is willing to allow so much that hinders us to be stripped away, including at times our health and well-being? Where do my beliefs of what well-being actually is not align with my Father's? It makes me wonder. It also fills me with wonder that our God is so determined, so cunning, so persevering, and so good that He will fight for our hearts through every moment and situation of our days that we might know Him. For it is not in health that we find joy. It is not in living without pain of any kind. No. It is in His presence that we will know the fullness of joy. As Graham Cooke said, "The Father does not give us joy. He gives us himself. He is absolute joy personified."[2]

Let that sink in. *God doesn't merely give us joy. He gives us Himself.* Joy incarnate. And we are able to receive more of His presence when our hands and hearts have been uncluttered and purified by fire. Oftentimes that purifying hurts. But none of it is without a greater good. And whatever is going on within our lives or around them, we can live with a heart that is expectantly waiting. A heart that is grounded in hope.

"May the God of hope fill you with all joy and peace as you trust in him, so that you may overflow with hope by the power of the Holy Spirit" (Rom. 15:13).

Dinner

Last summer, when all my family was going to be home at once, I decided to surprise them and make a large dinner. A lot of thought and planning went into it, a lot of preparation. I set the table in a special way. I got out candles and lit them. I laid pretty placemats on the table and matching glasses. I made a special salad—meaning I didn't merely rip open a bag and dump it into a bowl as I usually do. No, I chopped things. I even prepared a fresh homemade dressing. Making dinner took a lot of time and a lot of slicing, dicing, sautéing, and baking. Oh, the house smelled delicious.

My sons knew when to be home for dinner. Dinner at our house, barring an act of God, is always at 6:00 p.m. Has been for all their lives. So they came home with plenty of time to spare, but they had been so hungry that they'd stopped at

Chipotle an hour earlier and eaten massive burritos. They were filled to the brim.

They didn't know I had gone to a lot of extra work, that I was offering not just food but love to them that evening, so instead of coming home filled with anticipation, they came with no appetite at all. They weren't hungry, and though we still gathered together at the table, the beautiful, hard-won food was barely touched. If I had told them what was coming, they wouldn't have eaten beforehand. If they'd known a feast had been prepared for them, they would have waited, expecting that soon they would be filled. No one in their right mind would stop by McDonald's right before sitting down to a Thanksgiving dinner.

The waiting can be hard when you are hungry, but when you know a feast is coming, you know that the waiting won't last forever.

Dear ones, the waiting is not going to last. But there is no shame in being hungry while you wait.

Waiting can be an experience of emptiness. Our hands are empty. Our desires unfulfilled. Our hearts feel empty as well.

In *A Book of Strife in the Form of the Diary of an Old Soul*, George MacDonald described it this way:

> 'Tis hard for man to rouse his spirit up—
> It is the human creative agony,
> Though but to hold the heart an empty cup,
> Or tighten on the team the rigid rein.

Many will rather lie among the slain
Than creep through narrow ways the light to gain—
Than wake the will, and be born bitterly.
But he who would be born again indeed,
Must wake his soul unnumbered times a day,
And urge himself to life with holy greed;
Now ope his bosom to the Wind's free play;
And now, with patience forceful, hard, lie still,
Submiss and ready to the making will,
Athirst and empty, for God's breath to fill.[3]

The only way we can wait is if we are holding fast to the hope that we will not be waiting forever.

Waiting requires trusting. We will be able to wait with expectancy only if we believe that a great good is coming. It's an exercise of faith. It's an opportunity for our desires not to be quelled but to rise, for our hope to become heavier, more substantial, anchored more solidly in the belief that a goodness beyond our wildest dreams will come to us when our Jesus arrives in glory. And He is coming. We are promised His ultimate return, when He will put every enemy under His feet.

And even now Jesus is coming. He is present in the waiting. We do not wait alone. We do not wait in vain.

First Samuel 22 tells of the time David was hiding in the cave of Adullam from the vigilant search of King Saul. Saul, out of his mind with jealousy, breathing threats and hatred, wanted David dead. Prior to Saul's spear-throwing rampage,

David had every reason to believe his life would be going much differently at this point. He served the king. He honored him. And he fought bravely for Israel in the king's name. But Saul hated him more passionately with every victory and righteous act he did, and David eventually became a fugitive hiding in the wilderness to save his very life.

I've heard the story several times and imagined that David and his mighty men spending time in the cave were like scouts on a camping trip. A few days. A week maybe. Roughing it for a little while, but with an ebullient fellowship of Tom Sawyer-ish fun. But no, they weren't hiding for days or weeks or even for months. They were hiding in the cave for years. *Years.* David had been anointed the future king of Israel many years earlier. What had happened to that? How was this a part of God's plan? How long was he going to have to wait for things to go his way? Where was the good that was promised him?

Despite how things may have seemed, God had not abandoned David in the cave. He was training him. He was creating in him a heart that could rule. In the time of hiding and lack, when the world David trusted had not only failed him but turned on him, God was present and forging goodness in him. David's life was not ending or stagnant. Rather, he was becoming something the natural eye could not see: the greatest king Israel had ever known.

We know he was being formed, transformed really, because of two things. One, because God is faithful to keep His promises, and two, because in that place of unknowing, in that place of hiding, in that place of *waiting*, David worshipped God. It would have been natural for him to despair and start growing suspicious of God, but no—he continued to wait with expectant hope. In fact, it was in the cave of Adullam that David wrote Psalm 57.

> I am in the midst of lions;
> I am forced to dwell among ravenous beasts—
> men whose teeth are spears and arrows,
> whose tongues are sharp swords.
> Be exalted, O God, above the heavens;
> let your glory be over all the earth.
> They spread a net for my feet—
> I was bowed down in distress.
> They dug a pit in my path—
> but they have fallen into it themselves.
> My heart, O God, is steadfast,
> my heart is steadfast;
> I will sing and make music.
> Awake, my soul!
> Awake, harp and lyre!
> I will awaken the dawn.
> I will praise you, Lord, among the nations;
> I will sing of you among the peoples.
> For great is your love, reaching to the heavens;
> your faithfulness reaches to the skies.
> Be exalted, O God, above the heavens;
> let your glory be over all the earth. (vv. 4–11)

Like David, we cannot see the outcome of our lives from the darkened confines of the lonely cave we may find ourselves in. We cannot know the plans of God for us beyond His promises that He is working for our good at all times. And often we are far from comfortable as we wait. But, just as David wrote in the psalm, we, too, can remember God's great love and faithfulness and trust that our King is forging something beautiful in us even as we wait. He is making us into a people who will be able to fully partake of the feast He is preparing. He is making us into a people who will worship Him in the waiting, saying, "Be exalted, O God, above the heavens; let your glory be over all the earth!"

In our waiting God often deepens our hunger as well. A fabulous hors d'oeuvre is meant to awaken the appetite, not to quench it. It cultivates hunger by offering a hint of what is coming. There's a taste, a promise of being satisfied. Jesus awakens our longing for Him by using all kinds of things. He offers aromas of His goodness through His Word. He awakens our hunger through laughter, through beauty, joy, and connection. He quickens our longing in silence and solitude. He even increases our hunger through pain. Through sorrow and suffering, our longing for Jesus grows. He enlarges our hearts' capacity to wait with expectant hope through encounters with His loving presence as well as through times of loneliness and ache. We come to know Jesus in the waiting, not as one who is teasing out our time for some unknown sadistic reason but as the One who is sharing the experience of waiting with us, creating a union between His heart and our own.

Sometimes a melancholy ache will press against our hearts in our waiting, but we do not have to give in to despair. We'll feel the sadness, yes. But we can also tell ourselves the truth that, in Christ, the best is coming. We can live with expectant uncertainty, knowing that good continues to come our way even though we cannot see it. We don't know what is around the bend, but God does. And no matter what comes, we can know—we do know—that God will be there. He is our ever-present faithful companion on every road we take.

The day is coming, beloved, when our every hunger will be satisfied. Remember, "blessed are those who are invited to the wedding supper of the Lamb!" (Rev. 19:9). We are invited. The feast is being prepared. We can wait with the certainty of being filled.

Sadness

I was walking in the woods the other morning, surrounded by the green leaves of quaking aspen trees. The sunlight filtered down through the living heart shapes, making them reflect the light like stained glass. Their color, highlighted against the clear blue sky that was empty of clouds, seemed monochromatic; each leaf possessed the perfect hue of lime green. And then I looked more closely. I looked at the detail of one particular leaf and then another and saw that they were not perfectly, wholly green. Each held the telltale signs of a fallen world. Little brown dots flecked some. Others were captive to a border of gray. I could not find a leaf that was wholly one solid color.

And they were all beautiful. Together, the effect of the slight variations created a more interesting portrait, the touches of imperfection enriching the quality of the beauty.

And so it goes.

Joy is wonderful. Joy is ours. Joy is the currency of heaven. But being a person who is defiantly joyful does not mean being a person who is never sad. Like the brown invading the perfect heart-shaped green leaves of the aspen trees, we cannot escape the touches of sadness that speckle our lives. But being touched by sadness does not have to diminish the reality of our joy.

Friends, it has to be okay to be sad. Because we so often are. And of course we are. We, too, are constantly surrounded by the telltale signs of a fallen world. Every moment we love fades too quickly into the sacred terrain of memory. Every conversation that touches our soul with the joy of being known brings with it both a satisfaction and an ache. We know the conversation will end. We know that we are surrounded by boundaries that keep us from being fully known, from knowing fully, and from living with joyous abandon out of a heart that is fully free.

We are made for much, much more than this life has to offer us, and we know it. The soul's response to the ongoing awareness that this life will never fully satisfy is to ache. But we do not need to despair. We can ache with a grief that makes what is available all the more lovely. We can bear a sadness that enriches the tapestry of our lives, woven with its striking imperfections of beauty. Sadness can actually heighten our joy.

Sadness, by the way, is not the same thing as depression. And it is certainly not the same thing as hopelessness. Being sad is not a sign that there is something wrong with us but rather that there is something wrong with our world. It can serve as a stone of remembrance that we are made for more and that more is coming. It can elicit a holy response of mercy to others and of kindness to our own souls. Sadness is not a life sentence or an identity. We are not forever Eeyore. We are alive. And to be alive means that we will feel. We don't need to deny it, and we don't need to have it rule us. We dare not marry it to cynicism, and we must not fuel it with fatalism. It is not the end of our reality. It is instead a clue that we are strangers in a strange land. And we are passing through.

Sadness touches us all, but God can use it to enhance the beauty and joy of the lives we are living. Sadness can fuel our hope. It can arouse our expectancy.

Awakened by Longing

I woke this morning to my dogs calling me from their crates. Correction: I woke to Maisie, our two-year-old golden, calling to me from her crate. The occasional cross between a yip and a whine told me that I had fallen back to sleep and had been dozing too long for her taste. I'd been awakened several times in the night by an anxiety that threatened me. This past night, though, I had recognized it for the temptation it was: to take up a mantle of dark fear that was not mine to wear. I was too tired to wrestle with the spiritual assault. (That is what it was, friends. Even laden with some truth as to the circumstances of my life, it was a spiritual attack to entice me into the land of worry.) Too sleepy to corral my thoughts to the deeper truth of the faithfulness of God, I did not want to wake fully. I did not feel called to do so. This night, unlike too many other nights, I simply said no and then tucked my heart into God and continued to rest. I redirected my thoughts first to sweet memories, then to memories I wanted to make, and suddenly Maisie was calling to me. Surely it was well after 6:00 a.m. Sweet and poor girl. I looked at the clock, and it was eight! I quickly got up to let both of our dogs out to run and take care of business.

When I opened the door to release them, a cold blast hit my face. It was a crisp cold. A winter cold. A cold that spoke of past snow and past stories. I recognized a scent that I hadn't smelled for years. Though the winter here is full of crisp, cold mornings, something in the wind, or perhaps something in the night, awakened a stirring in my soul. I remembered that evocative smell, that feeling of an invitation to play.

Suddenly I was eight years old and wearing my favorite blue-and-white jacket with fur around the hood. I was a little girl again, getting ready to go outside and discover the joy awaiting me. I hadn't remembered that feeling or that jacket since I don't know when. Sense memory is something else, isn't it, showing up at the oddest of moments whenever the whim hits it. The sense of smell accesses and evokes memories more than any other.

This morning my grown-up self was still in my jammies when I opened the front door and was hit by the longing to be eight years old again. The door opened before me to a world filled with wonder and unending discovery. In my childhood I'd had different choices. Maybe I'd go sledding. Maybe I'd build a snowman. Maybe I would simply enjoy walking solitarily through the snow, relishing the sharp sound of crunching whiteness beneath my feet.

My soul was filled with expectancy all those mornings so long ago. I did not know what the days held, but I reached out to them boldly with both mittened hands. Back then I would dash out, unsure of what I would find but certain that it was worth finding.

This morning, so many years later, I remembered that feeling. I remembered the eager anticipation that once defined my heart. I remembered answering the invitation to live expectantly with an affirmative. To live without fear. I chose that then, and this very morning I had the opportunity to choose it again. I'd had the opportunity to choose it in the middle of this past night, and I am going to have a hundred opportunities to choose it today.

I pray to choose it. I pray that I will allow the memory to have its way with my heart.

I pray to become that hope-filled, expectant-of-good child again, and for the crisp morning air to have its way with me. For God to use it to cleanse me of cynicism, doubt, and fear.

I do not know what today will hold, but the fresh fragrance that enveloped me at the front door reminded me that I could be a woman of faith who welcomes it. So I will bundle up and take my joy-filled, always-expectant, and ready-for-a-romp-in-the-snow dogs for a walk.

Yes. I will do that. I will choose to be like them and hold dear the little girl I once was. I'm not going to spend my day running from the realities of my life. I am going to live it openhandedly with an eye out for the good that is coming my way today, letting it deepen my hunger. Hunger is not my enemy. It is a friend beckoning me onward to faith, to trust that in the waiting my soul is being enlarged for the purposes of God. And as I wait, I will worship. I will turn my gaze to Jesus and put my trust in Him. I will allow the longing to resurrect my hope that the One who promised is faithful and a great good is coming.

Eight

Thieves That Come

You will keep him in perfect peace,
whose mind is stayed on You.
—ISAIAH 26:3 NKJV

My least favorite mornings are the ones that begin in the middle of the night. Everything was fine when I went to bed. I wasn't worried about anyone or anything. Then, lightning struck from a clear, star-filled sky,[1] and worry woke me with a sleep-stealing fierceness.

A situation at work had happened earlier. Decisions had to be made pronto. I needed to navigate these relationships carefully, but the side effect of hurt feelings seemed inevitable.

What had I done? Why hadn't I foreseen this and done something, anything, to prevent it? Now it required damage control, and I had better start scrambling at 3:00 a.m. Go back to sleep? What a ludicrous idea.

Worry. It has a haunting life of its own. Like a sticky black fog, it can envelop my better senses and render logic mute. Worry can bind me with its slippery and strong chains.

Too often, in the clutches of worry, I don't even remember to pray, and when I do I throw up general prayers of "Help!" to God while simultaneously nursing the dire panic in my heart. The problems are *real*. They're *big*. There goes my mind again.

As you well know, praying about a situation, a person, a looming decision, or a failure is wise. The apostle Paul reminds us, "Be anxious for nothing, but in everything by prayer and supplication with thanksgiving let your requests be made known to God. And the peace of God, which surpasses all comprehension, will guard your hearts and your minds in Christ Jesus" (Phil. 4:6–7 NASB). The more specific I am about the details I am concerned with as I pray, the better the results. My hands unclasp, and I can picture the overwhelming fog of concern evaporating in the capable and sure hands of my Father. But if I grasp my worries tight and don't release them, I won't know the promised peace. Without yielding my concerns to God, I won't be able to access the joy I am meant to know even in the middle of the night.

A Den of Thieves

Fear. Pressure. Comparison. These are just a few of the forces to be reckoned with that steal our joy, and who among us is not familiar with each of them? They may be dark wisps floating around the perimeter of our lives, or they may be menaces that hold our hearts captive. All of them can lead to our hearts inhabiting a land far from the fields of joy we are meant to live in. Panic attacks are no joke. Anxiety can debilitate a person. Fear can press a heart down to immobility. Worry can consume a person. Pressure robs even the possibility of joy. Each one stems from a mocking and doubt-filled fear that we are not enough, that our lives are not enough, even that God is not enough to handle whatever difficulty we are currently facing. These and other thieves suck the life right out of a person. When under their crushing weight, having joy feels impossible.

Shame researcher Brené Brown wrote, "It's our fear of the dark that casts our joy into the shadows."[2] These fears, these robbers, are not yours alone to battle. You *are* a unique human being, but this struggle isn't what makes you so. If these thieves of joy were not common to all mankind, then Scripture would not have needed to warn us so strongly about them and instruct us on how to overcome them. But instruct it does. Over and over and over again.

- "'Therefore do not worry about tomorrow, for tomorrow will worry about itself. Each day has enough trouble of its own.'" (Matt. 6:34)

- "For God gave us a spirit not of fear but of power and love and self-control." (2 Tim. 1:7 ESV)
- "'The one who listens to me will live in security, and will be at ease from the dread of harm.'" (Prov. 1:33)

We are not to live in dread of harm. *Dread* means "great fear or apprehension."[3] We know we live in a world where horrible things can and do happen, but God wants us to live trusting Him and knowing that, whatever happens, He will care for us. We are not meant to live constantly on guard and braced against harm coming. We are to live with our hearts resting in the safety of God, which comes as the result of listening to Him and doing what He says. And that includes casting our cares on Him.

Does it feel scary to voice those fears you harbor in your heart, even to God? I have great news for you. You not only can do it; you are invited to do it. God knows them already, and saying them out loud can begin to deflate their power. Your heart can begin to rest in the truth that the worst possible thing that could ever happen to you cannot ever possibly happen to you.

It's true. I'm serious. What is the worst thing that could ever happen to you? Honestly, it is that you would be separated from God forever. That you would not live in His love. Think on that. Then remember:

For I am convinced that neither death nor life, neither angels nor demons, neither the present nor the future, nor any powers, neither height nor depth, nor anything else in all creation, will be able to separate us from the love of God that is in Christ Jesus our Lord. (Rom. 8:38–39)

God displayed His fierce, constant love for us once and for all on the cross of Calvary. The essence of His heart is no longer up for question. Because of all that Jesus won for us and our choice to receive it, God promises that we actually have nothing to fear.

So I will say it one more time, because we need to hear it: the worst possible thing that could ever happen to you cannot ever possibly happen to you.

Now that's something worth rejoicing over.

Joy Is Opposed

"We must go through many hardships
to enter the kingdom of God."

—ACTS 14:22

Living with defiant joy is not easy. Defiant joy is opposed. Perhaps that should be the title of this book. We all know this opposition keenly. Choosing joy can feel like pushing a massive boulder up a steep hill, impossible without the help of others. But if we were not meant to walk in and know joy intimately, why would God have commanded that we do so? We are prodded, invited, and instructed to have joy even in the face of loss, suffering, and pain. In many ways, it's a call to live in the realm of the miraculous. Of course, following this call, along with every other move toward the life God wants for us, means we will be opposed.

And behind all opposition, there is one who opposes. Behind all thieveries, there is a thief. Remember what Jesus said in John 10:10: "The thief comes only to steal and kill and destroy." Satan comes to rob us of our joy, our peace, and our connection to and faith in God. He whispers lies to us when we are vulnerable and does his best to warp our perception of our lives with his depressing and evil spin. His endless attacks can wear a person down if they aren't aware that the perceptions being suggested are coming straight from hell.

Satan is very good at stealing. He's devoted all his malice to separating us from intimacy with our good Father and the experience of deep joy that comes straight from Jesus' heart. The evil one uses the circumstances of our lives and of the world to bring discouragement and despair. That is why we must remember that though happiness is rooted in our circumstances, joy is rooted in eternity.

We were born into a world at war. It manifests itself in a variety of ways, but all of them come against our union with God. All of them steal our joy. We are not to live in fear of the war, but we are to be armed and shielded in the power of God, living with wisdom and awareness in it.

Our hearts need to be grounded in the unchanging truth of the love of God so that the manifold thieves that come our way do not have their way. In order to press on to the life Jesus has won for us and calls us to, we need to be aware of the enemy's schemes. We need to remember—even when we are weighed down by the worries, demands, and pressures of life, even when we feel that we are failing in them—that the Father invites us to rest in His arms and find reassurance in His heart toward us. His heart is only and always a safe place for ours.

Pressure to Come Through

"Even to your old age and gray hairs
I am he, I am he who will sustain you.
I have made you and I will carry you;
I will sustain you and I will rescue you."
—ISAIAH 46:4

My friend's lone tear had reached the bottom of her stony cheek, a solitary expression of anguish, all that her self-restraint would allow. Her countenance remained unmoved, and then her lips quivered, a crack in the immense self-control she was exerting to hold back the dam of her tears. She didn't yet trust me with the flow. Perhaps she didn't yet trust herself. If the dam broke, the flood would come. The full weight of her longing and pain would be evident and then would have to be engaged.

I knew my friend well. I knew the depth of her pain. I

knew what that one tear cost her. And it broke my heart on her behalf.

She was in pain. She feared that the story of her life had taken an irrevocable twist.

I hurt for her. I wanted to intervene. I reminded her of the truth and encouraged her to bring it all to Jesus. But I felt as though I could do nothing else for her. She was sinking, and I knew I could too easily go down with her ship. And that wouldn't help either of us.

God does call us to weep with those who weep and to rejoice with those who rejoice, but even as we weep with others, we do have to be careful not to get caught in their downward spiral. How do we avoid losing sight of joy when one we love is mourning? How are we to continue doing well in our core when one close to us is not doing well at all? Sometimes we need to lovingly extricate our souls. We need to practice benevolent detachment.

Benevolent detachment on behalf of others is more than just a theory. It's an imperative. Yes, we should care. But we cannot fully carry. Only God can do that. And He loves to carry, to rescue, and to intervene. We may be weak and inadequate to shoulder the load, but when we turn to Jesus and give it to Him, He reveals His strength to those we care for.

I am learning that when I feel as though a person's well-being is completely up to me, then I have taken on more than is mine to carry. There are times when I am meant to intervene on a person's behalf, and there are times when I am meant to walk alongside someone in caring support. I love those times. But the need for boundaries is real for all of us, and we will never be able to establish them within our own souls if we feel pressured to come through for someone beyond what God intends. When we are weighed down by the pressure to come through on another's behalf, joy flies out the window.

I tend to believe that it is my sole responsibility to help people, but then I remember God. I remember that He is good. I remember that He is a God who intervenes. He is the God of all hope. He restores what is lost. He can care for my friend. He can turn this around. He is always moving on our and others' behalf, much more than we can see in any given moment. He is much more capable than I am. Yes, I want to partner with Him in bringing healing and life, but I need to follow His lead.

So I pray for and then release my friend to God. I remember that I am not the one responsible for her; God is. Though I love her, my becoming worried and depressed on her behalf is not going to help. Truly loving her means I must detach my soul and allow my hope for her to rise. My joy cannot be rooted in any other person's well-being, and my possessing deep joy in the midst of another's pain does not diminish her sorrow or my love for her. I am meant to trust God deeply and entrust Him with all my cares. Even my care for those closest to me. Benevolent detachment breeds the possibility of joy.

Honestly, becoming a more joyful and free person can feel irresponsible. It certainly is difficult. If it were easy, then everyone would do it. Think of the most joyful person you know. What is it like to be with them? How do they respond to good events when they occur? What about when disappointment happens? Naturally joyful people feel disappointment and pain just as deeply as the rest of us. In fact, they are usually sensitive souls who feel most emotions even more keenly. But they possess a buoyancy that propels them to the surface when a wave of sadness strikes. They go down. They just don't stay down for long.

Truly joyful people are not flippant. When bad things happen, as they so often do, their mantra is not an empty "this, too, shall pass." They don't simply toss their heads and begin to make lemonade out of the lemons that have been supplied. The truth may be that "this, too, *shall* pass," but it will need to make its mark on us if we are to grow into the kind of people God is crafting.

Depth of character doesn't come easily. It doesn't come at all to those who refuse to admit that the difficulties in their lives are painful. It comes when we fix our gaze on Jesus and the reality that this life is only part of the grand scheme of things. Our Father has not lost sight of us, nor of those we care for. No problem, no pressure, and no situation is too big or too difficult for Him.

Comparison

We talked about the danger of comparing ourselves to others in chapter 5, but it is so common a thief of joy it bears revisiting.

I have a friend who will be visiting me next week. I can't wait. I love this woman. She's an accomplished writer, mother, grandmother, and wife. She's fit and takes good care of her body. And she has a deep relationship with Christ. I love all these things about her, but I often struggle with comparing myself to her, which then makes me pull away and retreat from offering my love.

Once, while walking behind this friend on a hike and observing her tiny frame, I asked her, "Are you a size zero?" She didn't answer. She did not like the direction of my question, sensing that an unhealthy comparison was taking place. She was correct. I continued, "How did I become friends with a woman who is a size zero?" Sometimes I say the stupidest things.

Though we do share many things, which is what drew us together in the first place, in many ways my friend is very different from me. I don't do the things that she does. I don't fly-fish. I don't paint, and I don't cross-stitch pillows that I designed myself. I don't minister to prostitutes on the streets of my city. I don't teach at the graduate level on deep heart issues. There is so very much that I don't do that she does.

I'm not her.

Comparing myself to her, I become intimidated by the glory of her unique life. I can feel my heart pull back. She's amazing. What have I got to offer her? My soul begins a downward spiral of self-loathing. And then the Holy Spirit nudges me to stop it and to consider what she would say about me. Her list of things she loves about me, because she sees what

I so often don't, would be as long as mine is for her. She sees my glory and how the fact that it is different from hers serves to enhance our friendship rather than hinder it. I want to learn from this woman. I want to glean inspiration from her passion. I want to offer her my friendship and build her up in the faith and the beautiful ways she expresses it. Comparing my life to hers, I come up short, and the distance between us becomes too far. It does not lead me to love well and focus on her but instead to pull away and focus on myself.

Sarah Young writes: "One thing that traps you in self-absorption is being overly concerned about how you look—in the mirror or in the eyes of others."[4]

I love learning from other people. Watching how a person interacts with others often instructs me on how I can interact more wisely and lovingly myself. Seeing how another honors her husband, parents her children, organizes her schedule, or prioritizes her relationship with God gives me examples of how to live my life more fully. I learn from others' lives and words, their teaching and instruction. I am meant to. But I am not meant to move from learning from them to belittling my need to learn. Another person's greatness does not mean I cannot excel as well. There is room in the kingdom of God for everyone's gifts to flourish. Rather than looking at other people's lives to validate my own, I'm supposed to be looking at the love and delight in Jesus' eyes. God values each and every one of our lives. We are unique and different from one another, and we are meant to be. If we don't live and love and offer in ways we are gifted to do, even if we're still growing, then the world will be missing what is ours alone to offer.

Resentment

Many years ago I was invited to high tea to celebrate my birthday. I was so excited! As a mother with young children, going out with another adult sans little ones was a rare occasion worthy of fireworks. The friend who invited me had made reservations at the special British bake shop in town known for its delicious sandwiches and scones that came on a tiered platter of decadent plenty. I hired a babysitter so I would have a few worry-free hours to talk and enjoy the company of my friend. I got dressed up and waited with eager anticipation for her to come pick me up.

She never came. When I called to find out if something had caused her to run late, her husband told me she was at the grocery store. She had forgotten the tea. She didn't return in time for us to go.

Being disappointed when people fail us or circumstances thwart us is a natural response. When we're disppointed, we've got to invite Jesus to bring His comfort, His perspective, and His love to help us be able to quickly forgive. Seventy times seven, remember? (Matt. 18:22 NLT). We have to be careful that our disappointment does not slide into resentment. Resentment is poison. Its presence is toxic to our own souls and to our relationships.

It's tragically easy to slip into resenting people, but this happens to us with God as well. Sometimes things don't go as planned or hoped for. Other times He seems slow to show up. We don't understand how He could let some things happen, and our doubt descends into resentment.

Disappointment is inevitable. Resentment doesn't have to be. Where resentment tempts us, the antidote is refusal. Where it has taken root, the antidote is repentance. And the fruit of that is freedom and joy.

Even in valid disappointment, trivial or deep, Jesus can bring more of His life, His goodness, and His redemption if we will invite Him into it. Invite away. He is forever faithful to show up. Especially when His character is in question. We've got to actively turn our hearts His way, rather than coming into agreement with negative or condemning explanations of the facts. Ask for His interpretation. Ask to see with His eyes.

For me with the tea, my thoughts sank into quicksand when I was too quick to believe that I wasn't a priority to my friend who forgot our date and therefore forgot me. My thoughts slipped down further into believing that there was no one to whom I was a priority. Suddenly I had no friends. I wasn't worth remembering. I was not good at doing friendship. My heart sank, and my disappointment turned to resentment at my friend for not caring about me. But that was not God's interpretation of the situation at all. The truth was, my friend was a harried mother herself. The demands of running a household had gotten the better of her in that moment. Her lapse in memory had nothing at all to do with me or how much she valued our friendship. She had simply been overwhelmed by life and lost track of her calendar.

When disappointment crops up in your life, ask God for His perspective. Oftentimes things are not as they seem at first. Do not allow bitterness to fester in your soul. It's more than a thief. It's a killer.

Pain

As I mentioned before, chronic pain has been bringing me to the mat lately. I can barely walk, moving only slowly with great pain. Parking more than a few spaces from the door of a store I must enter brings me to tears. I cling to grocery-store carts with the desperation of the drowning. My heart feels pinned down and reels with questions. *Why is this lasting so long? What am I doing wrong? Why isn't God healing me?* I'm beyond tired of it. Any and all movements are painful. And another thing, how come my doctor didn't give me a handicapped sticker? It would have helped so much. Questions abound.

Add to that the fact that my children are in a hard place. I want so much for them, for their lives, their relationships, and their walks with Jesus. Life deals hard blows to everyone, and they have been dealt them. Not out of sin. Not out of poor choices. But out of a fallen world. Sorrow. Loss. Heartbreak. And my heart is heavy for them.

On another side, a dear friend is suffering the pain of betrayal. Her oldest and dearest friend has chosen to walk away from God, finding solace from her disappointing marriage in the arms of another. She has rejected my friend, cutting her off completely, because she does not want to hear her adultery named nor the invitation to come back to Jesus, pursue counseling, or get help for her hurting heart. Sorrow haunts my friend. She wonders how she could have loved better.

Other friends, beautiful inside and out, bear the weight of rejection and loneliness. They feel unseen, unpursued, unfought for. They thought their lives would look much different from how they have turned out so far. Single. Childless. Divorced. Left. I don't understand why, and as much as I might wish I could, I can't conjure up someone to come alongside each of these dear friends for them to love and to love them back as they so want and deserve.

And yet.

A woman recently wrote me, saying:

This morning I awoke, feeling like my spirit had been wrestling throughout the night. I asked the Lord to speak to me, and I heard Him ask me to surrender to Him. I thought I had. But I think the truth of what is in my heart is more about how I find myself "tolerating" His will for me instead of coming to rest and embrace something I don't understand and wouldn't have chosen. There's so much we can glean from this set-apart time of what I call *sacred pain* . . . perhaps a deeper understanding, a new voice, a broader grace, and a fresh beauty that was hidden underneath that strength and comfort of what we have always depended upon. May we learn more steps to the dance with Jesus, and encourage others to join in.[5]

There is something forged in all of us that can only be forged through fire. Perhaps intense periods of struggle, pain, betrayal, persecution, and rejection are the times when the baptism by fire that Jesus talks about occurs. When we cling to Jesus and proclaim He is good in the midst of the licking flames, our spirits rise in a strength that is proven unshakable, and God is glorified beyond reckoning. Our pain becomes the terrain of God. It becomes sacred. Finding the good, or rather *choosing* to find the good, is choosing to align oneself with the Spirit of God who is always working toward our good.

It's more than a matter of focus, but it can begin there. It's different from denial; it is not turning your face away from the sacred pain but embracing God in the midst of it and finding that in embracing Him a greater good comes than you could have imagined. You become grateful *in* the pain, because you found Jesus with a crystal clarity heightened by all that has cut you to the quick. With that posture, you can become free from pain's deadening, life-stealing grip. In that place of freedom, our joy remains intact, planted firmly in the goodness of our Father.

In 1 Thessalonians 5:18 we are instructed to give thanks: "Give thanks in all circumstances; for this is God's will for you in Christ Jesus." Perhaps it will help us to give thanks when we know that even in the darkest of nights when we cannot see, we can trust that the God of love is forging gold in our hearts. It is a gold that cannot be stolen by any thief, no matter how desperately they may try.

A thief's power to steal is deemed impotent in light of our powerful God. Fear in its manifest forms is dismantled by the overwhelming love of Jesus. Our worries are quieted in the constant presence of the One whose name is the Prince of Peace. We will not be overcome because Jesus has already won our victory. The only thing that will overwhelm our hearts is the revelation of the immeasurable, boundless, all-consuming love of God. The thieves lose. Their presence can taunt, but the fruits of their taunting—when we turn our gaze and present our needs and our hearts to Jesus—are opportunities to worship. Joy comes. Joy indeed comes.

Dear Father, in this moment, I give You my worry. I give You my fear. I give You my anxiety. I give You all dread. I lay it all in Your hands. I open my hands to receive Your love, Your power, and the mind of Christ. I receive Your peace. I receive Your promise of faithfulness. I trust You. I trust You with my life and with the lives of those I love. I trust You with my future and with theirs. I choose to look at You and not my circumstances. I repent of comparing my life, my looks, and my abilities to others. I choose right now to rest in who You have made me to be and all You have given me. Thank You, God, for my life. Thank You for creating me uniquely. I confess that I am wonderfully made. I announce that greater is He who is in me than he who is in the world. I agree with Your Word that proclaims You have given me every spiritual blessing in the heavenly realms in Christ Jesus and that You will supply all of my needs. You are my enough and You are enough for me. I love You. I praise You. I desire to live this day and all my days in union with You. So to that end, I give everything and everyone to You—so that I may have You.

It's in Jesus' name I pray, amen.

Nine

The Signs All Around Us

Joy is the infallible sign of the presence of God.
—Pierre Teilhard de Chardin

I hate endings, and today is the last day of our weeklong summer vacation. It has been filled with mornings lingering over coffee and slow days empty of responsibilities. Restful evenings have been free from preparing for the next day's duties, and all day long the requirements that usually make up my life have been far, far away. A galaxy away. The weather has varied from baking heat under cloudless skies to the majesty of violent thunderstorms. The wind has been still, and the wind has knocked over trees. The full spectrum of it has been wonderful.

This morning, as we were packing up to head back to our regular life, lyrics from an old Joni Mitchell song began to play in my head, "You don't know what you've got till it's gone."[1] *Did I make the most of these days?* I wondered. *Did I drink in all the beauty I could? Did I get all the goodness from it that was available to me? Did I waste it?*

Questions like that make my heart sad. I am tempted to think I missed it. I worry that I was given the gift of a week away and I've somehow squandered it. But of course I did, and of course I didn't. I can't possibly be keenly aware of all the beauty around me at all times. My soul isn't large enough or attuned enough yet to take it all in. Neither is yours. So I am choosing right now to believe I haven't blown it. I have received the gift of this time to the best of my ability: resting, reading, praying, talking, and being silent. I feel so much more refreshed than when we first left home, but I also feel more prepared to enjoy a banquet and I've only just had the first course.

I want more. The taste of rest and beauty has touched a deep longing in my heart but not sated it. Rather, I am more keenly aware of my hunger. I am afraid that by leaving I will also leave behind all the gifts I have received, that I'll have to go into a new season of starvation. I've done it before, headed back into the valley from the mountaintop experience, and just weeks later I'd completely forgotten the dizzying joy of the heights. I want to hold on to the goodness. I want to remember. I *need* to remember, because by remembering I am assured that just as God promised, there is still good coming. I didn't know these days would be so rich. I don't know what tomorrow will hold either.

I can look forward with hope while I also hold sadness in my heart that this time has come to an end. I can be gentle on my soul that truly grieves chapters' closings.

Because the truth remains that I hate endings. I don't believe our souls were meant to know them at the level that we do. The hound of heaven chases us with the truth of life, and the hounds of hell chase us with a mocking hiss that everything good will come to an end.

Last summer, at the close of another vacation, one that I shared with my sons and their wives, I was near tears. Did I mention that I hate endings? My son Sam and my daughter-in-law Susie were the last to leave. Sam is a sensitive soul, keenly aware of what is going on beneath the veneer of a happy face. As he hugged me goodbye, he quoted my favorite sentence from George MacDonald's *Phantastes*, whispering into my ear, "A great good is coming, Anodos, coming to thee."[2]

I caught a rising sob in my throat.

Endings are hard. They mark the close of a season. But they also mark beginnings.

The old has gone. The new has come. In fact, the old has to go in order for the new to come.

The school year begins, and the school year ends. Summer comes, and summer comes to a close. Christmas comes, and Christmas goes. The old year gets sung out with "Auld Lang

Syne," and the new year is rung in with fireworks. Winter holds the earth in its icy grip, and then a daffodil breaks forth, proclaiming its end. Spring blooms and summer scorches and autumn bursts and falls to the ground, and here we are again in the cold. We must pay attention to the story unfolding around us every single day. Life. Death. Resurrection. In Christ, no ending is forever.

Yes, for now, time marches on. Time here is our fleeting gift. I don't know how many days I have been given, and neither do you. But I do know that by spending them in regret, my fist clenched to hold on to the goodness I do know, I am prevented from receiving the good gifts that God has in store for me. God has given golden nuggets in the midst of the bleakest of times. He's been lavish. And He doesn't change. If He's been generous and kind and good in the past, won't He remain so in the future? Yes. Yes, He will.

As Sarah Young wrote in *Jesus Calling*, "The only thing you can grasp without damaging your soul is My hand."[3] We must hold on to God's hand. The time we spend remembering who He is, what He's like, and what He's done breathes life into our souls whether they feel green or frozen. And the time we spend letting His living Word wash over us infuses us with life and hope. It is the water and food that we all crave.

We need to remember the goodness that has been. We need to remember who God is and who we are to Him. We need to remember His promises. His promises help us to step forward with hope.

In C. S. Lewis's book *The Silver Chair*, Aslan the Great

Lion sends two children on a quest. To help them on their extremely dangerous journey, Aslan gives one of the children, Jill, four signs to follow and remember. She is to share them. Recite them. Speak them aloud. Remind herself of them before she goes to sleep and go over them when she first wakes. And most importantly, she is to follow them, for they are essential if she and her companions are to fulfill their quest and return triumphant. If she forgets them, it may cost them their very lives, let alone their victory. I told you their journey was dangerous.

So is yours.

We must remember the signs. The signs God has given us to guide us on our journey are different from the ones given to Jill, but they are just as vital. They come to us in the longing that rises up from seeing Christmas twinkle lights and feeling the wind that flows down from the mountains, beckoning us to climb. They are in the beauty of the song and the melody that echoes within you that you don't understand. They are the stories you love, the art that moves you, the music that stirs you, the playgrounds you escaped to, the smell of fresh baking bread that allures you, and the embrace from someone who feels safe.

They come to us in the promises of the Scriptures, and they continue to come to us every moment of our lives. They help us take hold of hope, beauty, and life and keep us moving forward no matter how difficult things may get.

When a vacation finally comes and when it is over, in the midst of celebration and in the middle of mourning, during times of great pain and through times of great joy, the call is to remember. This admonition flows throughout Scripture. Deuteronomy 8:18 tells us to "remember the LORD your God." First Chronicles 16:12 says to "remember the wonders he has done, his miracles, and the judgments he pronounced."

If we forget—no, *when* we forget—who God is, what He has done, and who we are in Him and to Him, we put ourselves in great peril. We cannot live well nor arrive at the end of our journey triumphant unless we remember.

Yes, there are many things that help us to remember. But one that constantly surrounds us—if we will have the eyes to see—is nature itself. Creation shouts the glory of the Lord. It speaks of His character, His power, His generosity, His presence. It tells us of God's beauty, His splendor, His majesty, and His goodness.

I was reminded of this last summer when we spent a week surrounded by the majesty of the Tetons. The deep blue of Jackson Lake holding the gaze of the immovable jagged lines of mountains grand. The otherworldly sounds of bugling elk, varied and haunting, weaving through the air. The magnificent bulls running to chase one another off in their annual challenge of strength. Summer at its zenith like a ripe peach ready to fall. Greens hinting of gold, the last fling of intense summer heat wild in its glory.

Natural beauty is more than a balm. It is a testament. Nature is God's Pinterest page, reminding us that joy is the greatest reality. That there is beauty that is deep and untouchable. That there are rhythms to nature and tempos to life. Goodness and truth prevail. The promises of God are eternal.

Sitting on our back porch the other morning, looking and listening as the quiet new day began, I was reminded again of all these things. I love the early morning hours. The stillness. The gentle breezes through the aspens. The light feet of a passing curious chipmunk. The flurry of a hummingbird as it wings its way to the feeder. Sunshine. Warmth. Beauty. God speaks through creation. And what does He speak of? Goodness. Presence. Intimacy. Care. Splendor. Strength. Tenderness. Love. Bounty. Magnificence.

The prophet Isaiah wrote, "The mountains and the hills will break forth into shouts of joy before you" (Isa. 55:12 NASB). Of course they will.

Most mornings I go on long walks in the hills near our home. It's my prayer time, my centering time, my sacred time with God before I enter the fray of my day. For the past year, due to my health, I have been unable to go on my walks and have been relegated to looking at the beauty of nature through my windows. But look I do. I am eager to be able to stroll again, to have the strength to walk and, in the future, even to hike. But it is a ways off yet. Though my soul finds nourishment in the wild garden of our Creator, for now I somehow must seek to have it nourished without being enveloped by it.

Did you know the average American spends 93 percent of his or her life indoors?[4] I'm stunned by that percentage. And that includes time spent in parking lots—simply walking from the car to the grocery store, the job, the school, and the house. Almost 85 percent of Americans never get out into the wild. People who, for a variety of reasons, do not spend time outside, let alone in the wilderness, are not exposed to green trees or open vistas or air free from the sound of horns honking and various radios blasting. Their lives are spent in the city, and their souls are spent in the desert. And it does them great harm. That's why whole ministries exist with the aim to get inner-city people, primarily children, out into the country. That's why gardens are tended in the middle of tenements. The soul needs green in order to green up itself. The benefits of time spent outdoors are manifold.[5]

Whether or not we are able to or choose to spend time in nature, drinking in the beauty and reminders of God that it offers, our souls crave nourishment, and we will find ways to be sated. Either with God or without Him. One way brings sustenance and goodness, the other only a deeper craving and then a wandering further away from the life we need. We must remember and follow the signs found in the Scriptures and in the glory of creation that point us to life.

All the signs point to the miracle of the cross: death comes, but it is followed by life. All our roads, too, will at times lead to crucifixion—of our own expectations of a pain-free, fulfilling, dream-come-true life. All of them. And when we reach that inevitable end, we reach the end of ourselves and are met with a choice. We can make a cynical decision that all life is empty promises and pain, or we can look for a deeper, higher fulfillment of our heart's true desires.

And those are met in the resurrection and hope found only in the King of kings, Jesus Christ. We are surrounded by the signs of the resurrection with every sunrise and every spring that comes our way.

There are promises for life. We have to know them and understand them. There are signs that point us to the expansive, immeasurably good heart of God. We must look for them. We must remember.

We need to speak them aloud. Share them with each other. Recite them to ourselves. Marinate our hearts in them. Tell them to ourselves before we go to bed and remind ourselves when we wake to the new day. We must remember the signs. We must remember our Jesus and look for the ways He calls our hearts to His:

We live in a love story. We are created for romance and we have an insatiable capacity for it. Now, God gave us such a heart; it was one of his first gifts to us. (You have to have a heart to live in a love story.) Then he gives to us this world that is so breathtakingly beautiful. "The earth is filled with the love of the Lord" (Psalm 33:5). You see it in the fact that he made grass just firm enough that it stands up straight like a carpet, but not too firm that it hurts you when you run on it with bare feet. And he makes snow just firm enough for snowballs and sledding, but not so firm that it hurts us when it falls; it falls so softly. He makes birds and their songs just loud enough to be delightful, and he creates our ear to delight in the sound. Do you begin to see the tenderness and the love of God through all creation? . . .

All of this is the love of God wooing you. Some of you found the romance of God at the beach. Some of you found it on the rivers or in the meadows. Some of you found it in books. All that has ever stirred your heart, that was God romancing you. For as the Bible says, "Every good and perfect gift comes down from the Father above" (James 1:17).[6]

We have to remember that the secret of joy is this: knowing that God is the love we are longing for.

Let us remember together.

Rhythms and Rest

Scrub oak covers the hills in the Front Range of Colorado. They are the last to leaf out, stubborn in their arrival come summer, and the first to fall in the blustery wind that signals its end. But, oh, they are marvelous. The soft virgin lime-green leaves that bud first are velvet to the touch. After so long a season of bareness, seeing them emerge causes my breath to catch in my throat. Then suddenly, when I'm not looking, they fill out, exploding with green. They soak up the sun with their abundant life and cover the hills like a carpet of emeralds. The canopy of deep summer is their lively playground. They provide cover for the spotted and gangly newborn fawns and a nesting place for the humming-birds, who make their home in the lush leaves as soon as they arrive.

Then comes a shift in the wind, a hint on the breeze, a coolness I feel but am not ready to admit to, and the leaves of the scrub oak begin to turn. First a slight hint of gold around the edges warns that, like nomads, the leaves will not stay long. Oranges and reds engulf the green next like hungry flames. It is the scrub oak's stunning swan song. An autumn patchwork replaces the solid sea of jade, and I know the quilt will not linger. In the Rocky Mountains, autumn falls as quickly from the landscape as a shooting star.

The wind blows harder. The leaves come down, dry now and brown, littering the landscape with their final goodbye.

The branches are naked then, the view through them no longer blocked. When the snow falls softly, it lands on the branches gently, dusting one side with powdered-sugar grace. On very cold days, they become embroidered with icy crystal lace. But, mostly, they are naked. Brown. Empty. It takes an effort to see the beauty that remains. Sometimes for me it takes a sheer act of will to bless them in their starkness.

They look dead. But, of course, in winter the plants are not dead at all, though they may appear so. They are slumbering. They are settling deep inside their brown limbs and resting so that they may burst forth again one day.

There are rhythms to life, just as there are rhythms in nature. I'm a summer girl myself. My soul greens up when surrounded by the burgeoning life around me. But even I, who dream of eternal summer, know that my enjoyment of it is both heightened by and dependent upon its chillier cousins.

Nature teaches us so many things, and its seasonal lessons should not be ignored. The slumber of winter. The promise of spring. The glory of summer. The bounty of autumn. The rhythms of repose and exultation, starkness and abundance, death and life—it all surrounds us for the ongoing purpose of reminding us of the truth about the nature and needs of life.

My husband is lying on the couch now, resting. It's been a full day of hard physical labor, following months of equally hard days filled with spiritual, mental, and emotional labor. This would qualify as his third nap today if I were counting, which I am. I love that he is getting rest. In John's seasons of busyness and hard demands, I long to create more space for God to come and tend to the deep places in his heart that so need Him. I pray for them for myself as well. Our lives have looked a lot like winter lately. We've felt like it. Our souls have grown cold and weary. And there is a gift in it. We are being invited to rest, to allow the roots of our souls to grow deeper into the rich soil of God's love in order to be strengthened and replenished.

The seasons are changing, my friends. Even as I write now, school has begun again. Yellow buses have appeared on the roads dotted with waiting children and anxious yet expectant parents. The golden leaves are beginning to be sprinkled in. Higher up in the hills, the yellow aspens outnumber the green ones. There are reds and oranges. Brilliant primary colors set the hills ablaze, magnified against the crisp blue skies.

And winter is coming. Indoor days of coziness and outside days of brisk air. Maybe a blizzard or two. No more flip-flops but snowshoes. Maybe the flu. Maybe warm soups and fires. Nights falling earlier. Darkness and cold and stars that shine all the brighter because of it, and the invitation to remember that our souls need to be nourished with rest. To remember that in every season, there is a unique beauty and the presence of God within it.

Nature speaks of the signs.

Pain in life speaks of the signs.

Celebrations speak of the signs.

I'm about to become a grandmother to a new little one, and I can't wait. All new life speaks of the signs as well.

We said goodbye to a dear and irreplaceable friend recently, and the pain of his passing speaks of the signs.

There is death, yes. But after death, there is life. There is winter, yes. But after winter, there is spring. There is the crucifixion, but after the crucifixion there is the resurrection.

Our God has gone before us into all things.

Our Jesus has suffered in every way that we suffer. He is acquainted with grief. And there is not a moment of your life—not even in the moment of your passing on to heaven—that you are alone. You have a faithful companion who goes before you and behind you, who promises to never leave you or forsake you. Who has promised that He has suffered in ways you never will so that you will have eternal life—the life that you have always wanted and were born to. Where your every longing will be fulfilled and your every dream will come true.

So in obedience and with hope, I am saying yes to the next season. I am speaking it out loud. Yes to the new. Yes to believing that God is good and has good in store. Yes to letting my sorrow at endings deepen my soul's dependence on Him. Yes to Jesus.

And so we all can say goodbye to seasons, to relationships, even to loved ones with an open hand and welcome every new season, knowing that good is coming and that good has won. Jesus, help me to do that. Help us all. Please. We trust You. Help us trust You, the only One who never changes, even more than we have before.

Because a great good is coming. Coming to thee.

Remember.

Ten

Cultivating Joy

Joy does not simply happen to us. We have to
choose joy and keep choosing it every day.
—Henri J. M. Nouwen

Winter is long in Colorado. The terrain outside our home feels every inch of its 7,000 feet of elevation. Early May hits the calendars, and gardeners sharpen their tools like soldiers preparing for an invasion. Till that soil! It's planting time! Actually, at this altitude, planting time isn't until May 15, but some eager beavers can't wait and ignore the time-tested date. Sadly most who do so end up planting again after that last surprise winter storm stealthily arrives and kills all fledgling attempts to green up the world. Me? I've learned that lesson too many times, so I wait.

Well, okay, I do plant a large pot. But it's covered (mostly) by our front porch, and I only plant hardy things in there, because . . . well, I just can't help myself. I need to plant! I need to cultivate beauty. Beauty of all kinds is worth nurturing. To cultivate is also one of the mandates of Scripture. Back in Genesis, God told Adam and Eve to be fruitful and multiply (Gen. 1:28 NLT). He calls both men and women to join Him in creating beauty of all kinds. The ability to create is one of the glorious ways we bear the image of our wholly creative God. He commands us to cultivate the earth and to rule over it and care for it. Cultivation is one of the gifts of God that we are meant to enjoy and share with the world.

Missionaries we know in Senegal, Africa, told us that when their Muslim friends became Christians, they began to plant flowers in their front vegetable gardens, to the consternation of their neighbors. Why were they giving up the valuable food-producing space? people asked. Because the flowers were beautiful, they answered. Their hearts needed to cultivate beauty in every way available to them. When people are emboldened by hope, they create beauty in a million ways.

Choose

When I was young, I thought that following God and being a Christian would lead to a life that was kind of easy, filled only with happiness and free from pain and sorrow. Silly me. I'm not even sure where I got that idea, except maybe from teachings spouted by TV evangelists who espoused a prosperity "name it and claim it" doctrine that was popular when I first chose to follow Jesus. It tickles the ears, doesn't it? It's so appealing, this thought that if you are a true believer you are spared suffering and gifted only with a positive existence.

It is also completely contrary to what the Scriptures teach.

If Jesus was perfected through His suffering, who are we to think we won't be perfected through the same means? (Heb. 2:10).

Now, don't get me wrong, Jesus came that we might have life and life to the full (John 10:10), and it's the joy of the Lord that is our strength (Neh. 8:10). It's just that this promised joy and life come to us in the midst of the easy *and* the hard, the triumphs *and* the travails. The key, then, is to intentionally cultivate that joy in our hearts—to choose it— no matter what season we're in, the easy or the hard. And life *is* hard a lot of the time. This world we live in is not Eden. We are not in heaven. Not yet. But, in the middle of this often difficult journey, God "has taken great measures to preserve our freedom of choice."[1] We have the freedom to choose to grow in joy or to retreat from it.

Said another way, life will inevitably be hard, and as maturing believers with our eyes set on Jesus, we will constantly be presented with opportunities to make choices that will either lead to a deeper joy or not. Here's what I mean:

It's hard to stand up against the group when they are going the wrong direction—spiritually or any other way. But it's also hard on our consciences afterward if we don't. That Jiminy Cricket won't be quiet.

It's hard to be kind to the mean, curmudgeonly neighbor. It's hard as well to be convicted later of being unloving.

It's hard to not spend the money on the item we so desire. It's hard to save money. It's also hard to be in debt.

It's hard to have a loving but tough confrontational conversation with a friend. It's also hard to not have one and then have offense and distance creep into that friendship.

It's hard to fight for a marriage. It's hard to lose a marriage.

It's hard to break an addiction. And it's hard to be captive to one.

It's hard to live under the cloak of depression. It's also hard to step toward healing.

It's hard to face the story of your life. And it's hard to live in denial.

It's hard to reject the pressure of other people's demands. It's hard as well to live under them.

It's hard to set aside time every single day to press into the heart of God. Sometimes it's even hard to pray. It's hard to find the time. But it's harder to live your day with strength, hope, and integrity if you don't.

It's hard to pursue Living Water. And it's hard to live in a dry and thirsty land without it.

It's hard to fight for and guard your heart. It's hard to lose it.

We get to choose our hard, and the decision we make will either lead to cultivating our hearts with a hope-filled joy or deadening them with weariness and despair.

Every morning when I wake up, I can guess that there are going to be hard things in the day. But the hard I choose is to follow Christ wherever He leads, and that hard leads to life and joy. Always. Even in the midst of suffering. So I urge you to . . .

Choose life.
Choose thankfulness.
Choose to obey.
Choose the good.
Choose joy.
Choose Jesus.

Hope

Joy and hope have a symbiotic relationship. Hope is the nutrient-rich soil in which joy flourishes. Without hope, there is no joy. And joy nourishes our hope. It is the fertilizer that helps us to cultivate ecstatic blooms.

The problem is that holding on to hope can be easier

said than done. As men and women living in a fallen world surrounded by imperfect people, we are well acquainted with the truth that "hope deferred makes the heart sick" (Prov. 13:12). And our hope has so often been deferred that to speak of a surety of hope may be the largest leap of faith we can take. In order for our hearts to trust hope, we need to know that a promise will be kept. And to larger or smaller degrees, our daily relational experiences have taught us the opposite. Unfaithful people abound, and the landscapes of our pasts are littered with broken promises.

We were promised an outing with our father, and though he assured us he would be there, he never showed up. We entrusted our friend with a secret she promised to keep, and the secret spread like the flu. We were told the world is a beautiful place, and then we learned of abounding corruption and imbedded hatred that shattered our illusion of goodness. We promised to love, honor, and cherish, and our beloved broke our heart as he or she made a break for the door.

How are we to trust hope? How do we dare to so recklessly risk?

By looking at the track record of the Person we have placed our ultimate hope in. Is He trustworthy? Are His actions noble? Is He consistent? What do we know of His character? I am speaking of the Trinity, of course: the Father who gave His only Son to die on our behalf so that we never would, the Son who gave up His life in obedience to His Father because He believed the joy that was set before Him was worth every bit of suffering He had to endure, and the Spirit who has sealed us in Christ with His pledge, His promise, and His presence to teach, guide, strengthen, and comfort us as we live each day.

We may be tempted to doubt the love of God in a season of our lives where He remains silent and feels uninvolved. We may even accuse Him of being callous. But when we do, when hope seems lost, the answer is to look at the cross. At the cross, God proved once and for all that He is for us, that He will hold nothing good back from us, and that He has paid the highest price to rescue us. He has promised that He will never leave us or forsake us. And, by looking at His track record, we know we can take Him at His word.

What Is Our Hope?

Our hope is meant to be the anchor of our souls, to keep us steady in the middle of the storms of life. It is set firmly within the truth that Jesus is trustworthy. He has promised us that He is returning and that, when He does, He will make all things right, all things well, and all things new. He will bring us home, to the true home our hearts long for.

"Do not let your hearts be troubled. You believe in God; believe also in me. My Father's house has many rooms; if that were not so, would I have told you that I am going there to prepare a place for you? And if I go and prepare a place for you, I will come back and take you to be with me that you also may be where I am." (John 14:1–3)

He who was seated on the throne said, "I am making everything new!" (Rev. 21:5)

We received Christ by faith, and we are meant to enjoy Him utterly. We are meant to know and experience joy and to live with the vibrant hope of the glory that is going to be revealed when Jesus returns. Dear ones, He is returning. Say it out loud. Remind yourself.

We can live with a defiant joy because our happily ever after is on its way. In Jesus our life is unending and, at the renewal of all things, the life we long for is coming.

Really. Honestly. Truly.

Yours is no ethereal hope of a next life spent floating in the clouds singing hymns while strumming a harp. Yours is not a future of standing at a distance among the gathering of saints crammed together in the throne room. Yours is not a future where you will be shamed by a giant movie screen replaying your every secret moment before a huge crowd who gasps at your sins. This is not an unending life where you will spend eternity doing something so other than what you now know and enjoy that you simply are unable to imagine it, let alone hope for it.

When Jesus returns, you will be transformed, but you won't be transformed into an angel. You will still be you.

Only made perfect. None of the struggles you battle with here will be yours to contend with any longer. Think on that. You will be finally and fully free. You will be all that you were created to be. Your loved ones, too, will at last be utterly and completely whole and free. Let hope rise.

A life is coming to us in which we will not even remember that we felt the pain. Imagine that—imagine your every heartache lifted from you so thoroughly you don't even remember having the sorrow or the reason for it. As my husband John wrote in *All Things New*:

> The joy of this will far surpass our physical relief. Think of it—if God would offer today to remove from you just one of your greatest sources of internal pain, what would you ask him to remove?
>
> And once it were gone, what would your joy be like?
>
> Oh my goodness—I would be a happy maniac, dancing in my underwear like David before the ark, running about the neighborhood like Scrooge on Christmas morning, leaping housetop to housetop like the fiddler on the roof. And if *all* your brokenness were finally and completely healed, and all your sin removed from you far as the east is from the west—what will you no longer face? What will you finally be? How about that for your loved ones—what will they no longer wrestle with? What do they finally get to be?
>
> We shall, finally and fully, be *wholehearted*—a wish so deep in my soul I can hardly speak it.[2]

To help you imagine your future, ponder this question: What are the first three things you'd like to do when you get to heaven? And after that, what do you *want* to do? Write books? Sing? Swim with dolphins? Learn to paint? Bake delicious goodness and invite others to share it with you? Whom do you want to talk with? Whom are you looking forward to being reunited with? Whom do you look forward to asking questions and getting to know?

What do you long to have returned to you that the enemy has stolen? What reward would you love Jesus to bestow on you? What do you long to say to the Father? What do you long to hear?

Think on that. Daydream about what is coming. Imagine. Let your hope rise and, along with it, your joy. What is waiting for us one day is very much as C. S. Lewis described it in his last book for the children of Narnia:

All their life in this world and all their adventures in Narnia had only been the cover and the title page: now at last they were beginning Chapter One of the Great Story which no one on earth has read: which goes on forever: in which every chapter is better than the one before.[3]

Only a deep hope based on a true understanding of what is coming will be an anchor strong enough to hold you through the storms of life. You must cultivate your hope if you are to live in joy. You need to think on what is coming. Remember the words of Peter: "Set your hope fully on the grace that will be brought to you at the revelation of Jesus Christ" (1 Peter 1:13 ESV).

Shades of Sadness

Because of Jesus, we have every reason to be known as people of deep hope and joy. But does that mean we are going to be running around singing and dancing and smiling every moment of our lives? Are you able to? Am I? Is that what it means to "rejoice in the Lord always; again I will say, rejoice"? (Phil. 4:4 ESV).

I hope by now that you know I don't think so. If we were only doing that, skipping around with glee, we would be a people whose character is an inch deep, refusing to live with honesty and integrity. Remember, hard times come, and you must be willing to be present in them and feel the sorrow they bring in order to have joy. Your capacity to feel the one affects your capacity to experience the other. The two are connected. A soul deadened to the pain of the world and to your own life is numb to the joy available to you as well. As George MacDonald wrote, "Beauty and sadness always go together."[4]

These days, I am experiencing joy increasingly. It sometimes feels like a fire in my chest. I have known my sorrows, just as you have. My temptation is to run from them, fearing that allowing myself to fully experience them will overwhelm me. They are a tidal wave, and I don't know how to swim. But then the sorrow refuses to be ignored or stuffed or numbed or run from any longer. I must stop and give it space, allow the sorrow and sadness a voice. To feel it.

Here's a secret: our feelings have a life span. When we allow ourselves to fully feel our grief—to embrace it rather than shun it—the feeling of relief and release comes more quickly than we could imagine. The wave shrinks. We are buoyed by it. The sea calms. And we realize we did not drown. It won't destroy us.

We were created for Eden, yet we live in the valley of the shadow of death. Of course we ache. That's normal.

It touches all our lives: The shades of sorrow. The loneliness of loss. The emptiness and accusation of unfulfilled desires. The shame we feel when we brush up against life not going as it was meant to in the most minor of ways. The agony that overwhelms when we encounter beauty and the ache that rises in our hearts feel mocking rather than hopeful. The desperate fight to enter a new day when you do not know how you will be able to survive it, let alone live it well. The questions that taunt. The doubts that surface. The unexplained pain. The knowledge that everyone you love and everything you enjoy continues to change before your very eyes, time slipping through your fingers.

There is a sadness that tinges even the best of moments.

It is a sadness that is real and not to be ignored. It is a sadness that can point us home.

Yes, there will be sorrow in the living. But even there,

we will have many choices to make: either to let our lives be defined by sorrow or to dig into joy. It is as Ann Voskamp said, "The secret to joy is to keep seeking God where we doubt He is."[5]

How do we cultivate a heart of joy even amid shades of sadness? How do our hearts develop their rhythm, becoming increasingly synced with the heartbeat of heaven? By cultivating a heart that is thankful.

Gratis

One morning, after a wakeful night, when I finally surrendered to the prospect of a sleep-deprived day and got out of bed, I noticed that my heart was feeling heavy. I checked in with myself internally to see where I was and was not experiencing joy, and I immediately realized that if I was experiencing it at all, it was so far below the waterline of my awareness that it didn't even register. I decided to take stock in the clear light of day, knowing that sunshine often melts away the shadows that loom like mountains in the night.

What were the thieves robbing me of my birthright of joy? My list began. It centered on personal failures and pain and quickly moved to relational heartaches and struggles. Sprinkled in there were some financial issues. I wrote out my list in my journal, and as the list grew I felt justified in my lack of joy. "See! Who could have joy with all these things going on?" I said aloud. I found relief in making my list, but I also felt the satisfying pull of some kind of unholy indulgence. It felt good in a way that didn't feel good at all. After I finished, the list was fairly long. But then, from some place deeper inside me, I pronounced it "hooey." Nonsense. Nothing.

The Spirit had reminded me that I have much, much more to be grateful for. The gaze of my heart was being sucked to very real worries and disappointments like a metal coin to a tar-filled magnet, black and sticky and thick. And in order to become free of it, I needed to make another list, a list of the many things I had reasons to be grateful for. It was in meditating on these things that I finally felt the sticky stuff of circumstantial sadness begin to thin.

Here's what I am learning: A grateful heart is a heart that is free. An ungrateful heart is a heart that is bound. Gratitude inevitably leads to freedom.

The root of the word *gratitude* is the Latin word *gratis*, which means free. If gratitude and freedom are connected etymologically, wouldn't it make sense that the two are connected spiritually as well? When we cultivate hearts bent toward seeing the good we've been given, it frees us from the sludge of negativity so we can experience joy.

God created us to be a thankful and joyful people. He formed us so intentionally that joy will only flourish in a soil rich with gratitude. In fact, without gratitude, we do not have the capacity for joy. God wired our brains in such a way that it is impossible to feel joy without a posture of thankfulness preceding it. According to research published in the journal *Cerebral Cortex*, gratitude primes the brain for positive emotions: it "stimulates the hypothalamus (a key part of the brain that regulates stress) and the ventral tegmental area (part of our 'reward circuitry' that produces the sensation of pleasure)."[6]

We are called to be thankful in everything. Not *for* everything, but *in* everything. And we must be if we are to experience the deep joy that is meant to dwell in the very center of our being. Thankfulness is the key that opens the door to the joy we are meant to walk in.

A grateful heart is a heart that is free. An ungrateful heart is a heart that is bound.

I'm picturing Eeyore here. Or Puddleglum. Neither sees the good but only the possibility for the worst. To them, disaster not only looms but is probably coming in the next moment. Their fictional feet are chained to the ground with a heaviness that binds. I recognize myself in them. To be free, I need to look back at my life and the lives of others and remember the faithfulness of God. Though sometimes it may feel as though it would take a miracle to be lifted out of the mire of worry and transferred to a place of gratefulness, the choice is ours to make.

Remember: "*Eucharisteo*—thanksgiving—*always precedes the miracle.*"[7]

Gratitude is the key, friends. Gratitude unlocks joy. And to be grateful, we need to remember the reason for our gratitude—we are grateful because we have been rescued.

Remember

John and I had the privilege of visiting Normandy recently. It was a pilgrimage to the American landing sites at Omaha Beach and Utah Beach, as well as the cliffs of Pointe du Hoc. Additionally, we spent a long time at Normandy American Cemetery, walking among the thousands of crosses and stars with reverence. It was a holy pilgrimage where we went to pay our respects to the men and women who so valiantly fought for the freedom of Europe. So many, so very many, had given the ultimate sacrifice of their lives.

The people of Normandy remember. They honor the sacrifice of the Allied forces. Thousands of young people, men primarily, gave their lives for a people they didn't know to fight for the overthrow of evil. Flags of the Allies continue to wave in the towns, celebrating those who fought to free them. Signs in restaurants proclaim, "Welcome to our Liberators." In the schools, the children yearly take field trips to one of the sites, the museums, or the cemeteries to pay honor and to never forget what was sacrificed on their behalf.

And the result of their remembering is gratefulness. The people are so thankful. The atmosphere is thick with it. Remembering the goodness of God in the midst of battle, suffering, loss, and sorrow bears the fruit of gratitude and a freedom of heart that is tangible.

It made me think of a verse from the book of Joel: "Tell it to your children" (1:3). And they do. Beautiful memorials that honor and remember their liberators dot the landscape of Normandy. Many bear the insignia "Lest We Forget."

It's a little like how the Jewish people set up stones of remembrance throughout the Old Testament, markers to remind them of God's faithfulness and intervention (Josh. 4:5–9). We need reminders like these in our lives as we seek to cultivate joy in the midst of sorrow. God has come. He is coming still. When we remember His faithfulness in the past, it gives us the courage to believe that the One who says He never changes will be faithful in our present situation and in our future.

Where has Jesus come through for you? Really. Take a moment and remember. And then write it down. Remembering fertilizes our hope. It makes our faith burgeon and bloom. It strengthens our belief in the promises of God that He is good and He is for us. Remembering fuels our joy even when surrounded by thieves who want to steal it.

Sometimes being a joyful person amid this crazy world seems impossible. Well then, let the impossible commence. Because one of the secrets to being defiantly joyful is that it has absolutely nothing to do with the circumstances going on in your life or your world. Defiant joy does not depend on feeling happy.

Defiant joy is solely based on the victory of Jesus Christ and all that He has won for you. It rests on the fact that you are completely and utterly loved and cared for. In Christ your life is inextinguishable. Undefeatable. Victorious. Worry, fear, panic, and dread do not get to hold your heart hostage in their viselike grip. Your heart is safely held in the hands of your faithful God who promises that a life of unending joy is your inheritance. It is coming. Jesus led the way. And though the way often includes disappointment, pain, betrayal, and sorrow, none of them get to have the final say.

Only God has the final say over your life. Your future is secure. Your Father is faithful. His promises are true. The unseen world is a far more reliable anchor than the seen one. Your trustworthy God holds you and all you love. You can choose to be immensely and deeply grateful for that, always. And gratitude is the breeding ground of joy.

⁓

Father, thank You. I truly have so very much to be thankful for. Thank You for all the many gifts You have given me in my life, including my life itself. Thank You for Your endless love for me. Thank You that You had me in mind before You even created the world. What an amazing thought that is. I can barely fathom it. How stunning is Your love. God, You are lavish with Your love for me and extravagant in Your many gifts to me. I pray to have the eyes to see them today—the ones coming to me through Your Word and through Your world.

Oh Father, thank You for sending Jesus in my place. Thank You for including me in Christ. Thank You for including me in his crucifixion and death.

Thank You for raising me with Him and seating me with Him at your right hand. Thank You for granting me His authority and for anointing me with the Holy Spirit. I receive it all with thanks and praise. Lord, let my gratitude be deep and real. Help me turn my gaze to the wonder of You. Establish Your love profoundly in my heart and let it give birth to an untouchable joy based solely upon who You are. You are my glorious King and I am forever Yours. I love You. I need You. I trust You.

It's in Jesus' name that I pray, amen.

Eleven

On Behalf of Love

"Love one another."

—JOHN 13:34

When Adam Lanza opened fire at Sandy Hook Elementary School that fateful day, two of the teachers, Victoria Leigh Soto and Anne Marie Murphy, used their bodies as human shields to protect the children in their care. The *New York Post* reported that the principal of the school, Dawn Hochsprung, "reacted like a lioness protecting her cubs. She ran out of the office and lunged at Lanza—and died when he trained his gun on her and opened fire."[1]

I am awed and so deeply grateful for valiant hearts like these.

Sacrifice my life? Lay down my desires? I can barely let someone else choose the movie we are going to watch. Sacrifice does not come naturally. Nor does laying down our right to take offense—becoming critical or even miserable—not even when doing so would diminish another person's opportunity for joy.

Yet Christ calls us to lay our lives down for the benefit of others. We are instructed to die to the self-life—a call so contrary to the times we are living in, it sounds laughable. This is the age of the Offended Self. My way or the highway. Entitlement reigns. Agree with me or bear the consequences of my wrath. People shred one another on social media for the slightest offense. Opinions are spouted as if every opinion matters as much as the next. We judge, and we think it's our right to do so.

God says it isn't. Matthew 7:1 says, "'Do not judge, or you too will be judged.'"

God commands us to love one another, to bear one another's burdens—not add to them. He tells us to put the needs of other people above our own and, in humility, to care for the well-being of others.

What does that have to do with joy?

Everything.

Our choices to love will either increase or erode the joy of those around us. Much to our surprise, our choice to die to the self-life increases our own joy as well. Dramatically.

We know we are commanded to love. What I'd like to point out is that one of the most marvelous ways we love is by choosing to live with joy. Our choices to pursue a joy-filled life have a snowball effect on those who inhabit our daily world. There are so many reasons for this. For one, it makes us a delight to be around. For another, living with joy is the most enticing way we allure others to God. I'd like to suggest that being a joyful person is one of the key ways you can honor God, love Him, and lay down your life for the benefit of others.

To Grow in Love Is to Grow in Joy

Bernard of Clairvaux, a twelfth-century French abbot, wrote in his book *On Loving God* that there is a natural progression for people in the way of love. He described the first degree of love as loving yourself for your own sake.[2] This is where our culture has landed—all the entitlement and the offense, the self before all else. I'm not sure it can accurately be called love at all. If sacrifice is the gold standard of love, then this stage does not qualify. Now, some dear souls skip right past this entry-level experience, and some sadder ones remain here all their lives. I don't believe you can know true joy here. At best these folks pursue happiness, but it is as fleeting as the smell of a new car.

The second degree presented by Clairvaux is loving God for your own blessing.[3] It is a step in the right direction, as the soul turns to Christ, but the focus is still on the self. This is the "what's in it for me?" version of a relationship with God. A person in this stage is a child in every way, wanting their cookies and milk, and God is the one in control of the bakery. I was stuck in this stage for decades; I fear I abide too much here even still. Most Christians do. Far more people are willing to sign up for the church's financial peace class than they are eager to increase their tithing (if they tithe at all). You can bet that classes on parenting, setting boundaries, and learning to take Sabbath breaks will fill far more quickly than classes on missions. The church has been forced to present itself as a place you can get your needs met for the simple reason that most Christians are stuck at the second degree of love.

But there is a higher way. The third degree of love is loving God for God's own sake.[4] At this stage, we come to love God for who He is, not for what we can get from Him. Further, we become His intimate allies, because we want to join Him in His mission on the earth. Here we enter the realm of joy known by those in the kingdom of God. Like Jesus, we find that our deepest blessing and joy comes through our union with the Father. His desires become our desires, His delights our own. What brings Him joy brings it to us as well. Our greatest pleasure comes in God's will being accomplished in us and through us. We mean it when we pray, "Thy kingdom come, Thy will be done in earth, as it is in heaven" (Matt. 6:10 KJV).

If you've read this far, then I know you want to choose this kind of love and joy as deeply as I do; you are even now making the choice. Yes, God, help us. Reveal Yourself to us.

We long to live in intimate communion with You. We will not know deep joy without it. Consider another writing of Clairvaux's, the hymn "Jesus, the Very Thought of Thee":

> *Jesus, the very thought of Thee*
> *With sweetness fills the breast;*
> *But sweeter far Thy face to see*
> *And in Thy presence rest.*
> *Nor voice can sing, nor heart can frame,*
> *Nor can the mem'ry find*
> *A sweeter sound than Thy blest name,*
> *O Savior of mankind!*
> *O hope of every contrite heart,*
> *O joy of all the meek,*
> *To those who fall, how kind Thou art!*
> *How good to those who seek!*
> *All those who find Thee find a bliss*
> *Nor tongue nor pen can show;*
> *The love of Jesus, what it is,*
> *None but His loved ones know.*
> *Jesus, our only joy be Thou,*
> *As Thou our prize will be;*
> *Jesus, be Thou our glory now,*
> *And through eternity.*[5]

Did you notice how Clairvaux wrote, "All those who find Thee find a bliss"? Joy unspeakable comes when we know our God intimately and live in union with Him.

Clairvaux believed there was also a fourth degree of love: loving ourselves for God's sake.[6] When I first read this, I feared it was a shift backward to the self-focus of stages one and two. But then I realized I cannot love God and hate myself. In this stage, we learn to love and have mercy for ourselves, because we are His creation and He calls us to honor and respect His creation. We come to acknowledge that everything He has made is good, including our own lives, our personalities. We give our bodies to Him as living sacrifices, and when we do, we care for them. We take seriously the command, "Above everything else guard your heart, because from it flow the springs of life" (Prov. 4:23 ISV), and so we protect and nurture our hearts as well. We don't abandon our dreams and desires in false humility but lay them down at Jesus' feet, awaiting His blessing and direction. We do not hate. We love and bless ourselves with the purpose of honoring our beautiful God.

As we climb the ladder of the degrees of love, so we progress up the ladder of joy. Our hearts are expanded by knowing the Father, Son, and Holy Spirit as the source of all goodness, and our capacity to know and experience joy expands as well. It is a beautiful progression. Yet I think there is another rung on this ladder: loving others for God's sake.

Choose Joy as a Choice to Love

Debbie's teenage daughter, Taylor, wasn't feeling well one Sunday morning. No fever—she was just a bit tired and feeling punk, as my mother used to say. So Debbie tucked her girl in bed and let her rest as she and her husband and their younger child, Ben, went off to church.

When the family returned home a few hours later, Debbie went in to check on Taylor. She was unresponsive. In a panic, Debbie screamed for her husband to call 911. The emergency response team came quickly, but in the hours that followed, Taylor descended deeper and deeper into a coma from which she never recovered.

Days later, Taylor slipped into eternity, passing away at the hospital on a cold spring morning bitter with frost.

Debbie knew that her daughter was safe forever in the arms of her Savior, but her own arms were empty. The pain in her heart swallowed her whole, and she slipped into an emotional coma of her own. Unable to stir herself from her bed, she spent the next months in her darkened room wrestling with God and her own inability to save her child. Her passion for life had been snuffed. It was as if she, too, had left the land of the living. Joy? It had passed away along with her beloved child.

Until one day.

Debbie's younger son, Ben, was not gone. He was alive and well and grieving the loss of his sister in his own way. He had suddenly lost Taylor and then, in the days that followed, watched his mother slip away from him as well. His sorrow was magnified, his fear left unchecked. Joy was out of his reach.

Desperate, Ben came into his mother's darkened room

and opened the curtains. He sat next to his mother and told her, "I am alive. I need you. Don't you love me anymore?"

The Holy Spirit grabbed hold of Debbie in that moment. Through her son, He convicted her to not abandon the family He had given her. She was called to love. She needed to love her family who remained, and in order to do that, she had to choose to live. She had to follow the call of Christ to press into the heartbeat of heaven and choose to believe that joy was still within her and her family's reach.

She got out of bed. She chose to love God even without understanding why her treasured daughter was gone. She expressed that love by obeying Him and loving others, starting with her family. She began by bringing flowers to their breakfast table. She reintroduced music to their silent home. She began to slowly and intentionally cultivate joy in her own heart. She sought help for her grief-filled depression and began to take baby steps to rekindle the joy in her family's life as well. Debbie continues to heal, and part of that journey includes leading grief recovery groups at her church. Her joy has slowly returned as she has grown in offering her love on behalf of others.

The kingdom of God is filled with paradoxes, surprises. We set out to find joy for ourselves, only to discover the greater joys waiting for us when we live for others. The reason I bring all this up is simply this: Quite often we cannot find reason enough to choose joy and pursue joy for ourselves. But perhaps we can find new strength when we realize how much it matters to God and to those around us.

Dennis Prager, a nationally syndicated radio talk-show host and author, wrote:

> For much of my life, I, like most people, regarded the pursuit of happiness as largely a selfish pursuit. One of the great revelations of middle age has been that happiness, far from being only a selfish pursuit, is a moral demand.
>
> When we think of character traits we rightly think of honesty, integrity, moral courage, and acts of altruism. Few people include happiness in any list of character traits or moral achievements.
>
> But happiness is both.
>
> Happiness—or at least acting happy, or at the very least not inflicting one's unhappiness on others—is no less important in making the world better than any other human trait.
>
> With some exceptions, happy people make the world better and unhappy people make it worse.[7]

If being a happy person is a moral responsibility, how much more so is being a *joyful* person? Happiness skims the surface; joy is rooted in eternity. We are commanded to be joyful not merely for our own benefit but for the benefit of everyone else in our lives!

Choosing defiant joy in the midst of heartbreak is not an impossible choice. Perhaps baby steps are all that are possible for you to take right now, each tentative foot moving toward the hope that Jesus will meet you in your sorrow and breathe life and joy slowly but ever so surely back into your heart. It is a choice that you make for your own heart. But it is a choice you ultimately make for the heart of God and the hearts of those you love. Let love compel you.

No Greater Joy

Sometimes my heart explodes with joy. In those moments, if I had a tail it would wag. Excitement bubbles over in my feet, my joy displayed with swaying size nines. I remember the first time I felt this way. It was my husband who lit the fuse that led to fireworks going off in my heart. It's a real thing, those. So is the inner explosion. I experience it as if my heart is bursting, and it comes to me only in the company of others. People do sometimes break my heart, but people also make me burst in the very best of ways.

Paul, in his writings about joy, detailed both how important it is to have joy and what the primary source of it is in our daily lives. He wrote that other people were what made his heart burst with joy as well. Paul's joy was made complete through the ones he cared about.

- Therefore, my brothers and sisters, you whom I love and long for, my joy and crown, stand firm in the Lord in this way, dear friends! (Phil. 4:1)
- Recalling your tears, I long to see you, so that I may be filled with joy. (2 Tim. 1:4)

• Your love has given me great joy. (Philemon v. 7)

In some ways, Jesus was the same. Remember in chapter 2, when we looked at what brings Jesus joy? The Scriptures say that Jesus rejoiced greatly. He was exuberant! Why? Because He passed His authority on to us. He shares His victory with us. Our partnering with Him in His Father's work was His source of joy. And we get to do the same. We get to share the joy of our Master (Matt. 25:21).

As we grow in love, as we ascend Clairvaux's stages, we find no greater joy than when we shift our focus to the things that bring God joy. Our hearts—one with His—become preoccupied with bringing other people further into His kingdom, into life with Him.

I well remember a phone call many years ago where the subject turned to spiritual matters. My friend, whom I had been pursuing, began to ask me questions about Jesus. The conversation deepened and progressed, and she moved toward God in true ways. More was to come, but when I got off that phone call, my heart exploded and gave way to me leaping and dancing around the house with a silly exuberance. I was praising God and rejoicing and thanking Him from the depths of my soul. I was so *filled with joy*! There is nothing that makes my soul burst with goodness more than sharing Jesus and having the person respond by choosing Him.

Sharing our faith brings a joy that resonates in the heavenly realms: Jesus said, "In the same way, I tell you, there is rejoicing in the presence of the angels of God over one sinner who repents" (Luke 15:10). Living our lives openly before others leads them to ask questions—especially if we are joyful. People become curious about the light in our eyes and the hope that we have. And when they ask about it, or when we step out in faith and share the reason for our hope before they ask, our lives rise to the highest purpose for which they were made. We partner with Jesus in the work of the kingdom!

Jesus calls us to make disciples, to speak of the Word, to share the gospel. That is the primary purpose of our lives here and now: to love God and to love others by introducing them to Love Himself. So, first, we need to know what the good news of Jesus really is, and then we need to ask for the eyes to recognize the thirsty ones and the courage to share the Living Water with them. Inviting others into a life with Jesus is simply the best thing in the world to do. Helping others find the freedom, healing, and life that Jesus came to bring is also the most loving thing we could ever do.

As Brian Hardin wrote in his book *Sneezing Jesus*, "May we always remain intertwined and collaborating with Jesus in His work in the world—the business of awakening a slumbering species and setting free those who are naked and flailing."[8]

We are all called to live. We are called to love. We are meant to know love ourselves and have it do its deep healing and sanctifying work in our lives. We are meant to know joy, to be changed by it . . . and then we are meant to spread it. When, by our acts of love, others flourish, our joy will burst forth in our souls like the sun breaking through the clouds on a cold winter morning heavy with frost. Let it thaw the places frozen in us. Let it draw others to the warmth of its life-giving fire.

Know God that you might love Him for Himself.

Agree with Him that you are worthy of love yourself.

Join Him in loving others as a way to love Jesus back.

You will know boundless joy when you do.

Twelve

A Hui Hou

Those the Lord has rescued will return.
They will enter Zion with singing;
everlasting joy will crown their heads.
Gladness and joy will overtake them, and
sorrow and sighing will flee away.
—Isaiah 51:11

This week, in every simple task of my day, I've felt as though I've been slogging through knee-deep mud. I've felt that way because slogging is exactly what I've been doing.

It's sorrow; grief is such a heavy thing.

A childhood friend of mine died suddenly while shopping

in Walmart. Two other friends received diagnoses of particularly vicious cancers. Desperate prayer requests came in from others I love for various heartbreaking reasons. And then I received a gut-wrenching call from someone close to me, sobbing out the news of the unexpected loss of her young son. Morning had come, and he simply didn't wake up.

I fell on the floor.

Grief will do that.

But from somewhere deeper than the reservoir of my tears, I knew that I would not grieve forever. In my sorrow, my tears mingled with my God's. As the salty waters flowed, the thick mud of grief thinned. Life-giving water overwhelmed the weighty slough, and though I was mired in muck I knew I would not remain there forever. Because though death will knock me down, I belong to the Resurrected One who knocked death down. Dealt it a deathblow, as it were.

Sometimes I wish I knew the future. I'd like to be prepared for those late-night phone calls and other harbingers of doom. I often think I'd like to know what is coming around the corner, but, honestly, I'm glad I don't. Such knowledge might just do me in. Still, somehow, all of our souls can bear more than we could possibly imagine as we walk through this valley of the shadow of death. Human beings are amazingly resilient and can adjust to circumstances both dire and horrific. As they sing in *The Prince of Egypt*, hope *is* hard to kill. Hope is breath. It is life.

Hope is essential to the human heart. It seems to be innate too.

People have risen to fight evil and oppression ever since it first invaded the earth. They've worked for justice, held on to hope while grieving atrocities, and responded with actions that both loudly and quietly proclaimed their honor. Sometimes they responded with music. African Americans gave birth to blues and gospel music and jazz, all rich with unique proclamations of dignity and freedom. Men and women formed choirs in concentration camps. The beauty of their harmony brought life and hope to the listeners. To the singers, it brought nourishment to their souls and the declaration of their dignity as human beings.[1]

These men and women rose above sorrow untold and offered beauty and life in its place, just as we are all meant to do. Their dignity had been assaulted. Their humanity stripped away. In the core of their beings, a resilient flame remained. They were, as we are, image bearers of the living God, invaluable, their lives worthy of honor and respect—endowed with something to offer the world to make it a better place, even in the worst of places. And when it was offered, whether with song or tangible beauty, or a flowering strength displayed in a thousand different ways, hope rose. And believe it or not, joy followed.

The Knife-Edge of Joy or Despair

When our son and his wife, Susie, told us they were expecting their first child, it is not hyperbole to say that my son's face shone like the sun with a boundless joy. I have never seen anything close to that look on his face. Well, maybe somewhat close. A young boy on Christmas morn ripe with joy and wonder comes to mind. But this? This was new. Joy mixed with pride combined with utter and complete happiness.

I screamed with joy. Then I leaped out of my chair and proclaimed my love—not to my daughter-in-law but to my first grandchild. I bent on my knees before the new mother and whispered my love through her belly. There were many joyful tears shed that night. There were toasts and prayers breathlessly spoken with awe. I proudly put on my tacky new purple T-shirt that said "Grandma to Be."

Oh, the happiness! Untold. Immeasurable. The curiosity about and complete love over this unmet little one was full.

Months later, I was out of state and about to begin the final session of a conference I was attending when I remembered to turn off my cell phone. As I picked it up, I saw a group text with a message from one of my sons to the expectant parents, telling them how sorry he was and that he was praying. *Sorry for what? Praying for what?* I wondered.

Of course you know.

Susie was in the middle of an excruciating miscarriage, the pain was intense. I couldn't breathe. My heart broke and my tears flowed as I, frantic with grief, searched the building for an empty room where I could sob.

I was able to get a flight home the next day.

Taking place at some mysterious intersection of development, a missed miscarriage is described as being more painful than childbirth. Agonizing hours later, she passed our first grandson, Patrick Samuel, named after his father.

We didn't welcome him into our arms. We buried him. My children have never known such pain. The light has yet to come back into their eyes. I will never forget my grandson, I will never forget my children's sorrow, and I will never forget holding my husband as he collapsed privately in grief—his pain magnified by his children's.

It was a pain born of love. It was a pain born of the weight of human dignity. It was a pain born of sorrow at the loss of a cherished grandson and the intrusion of a suffering that we could see shaping our children's souls even as it occurred.

I have known grief, and I have known pain. But seeing my son and his wife ripe not with child but with agony was something new to rend my heart. Holding them both as he silently wept and she cried in travail for the son they had loved and lost, whom they had wanted so desperately but who now was gone, I came to know something about the heart of God that I previously had not known.

The pain of loving. The risk involved for your own heart. The danger of giving your whole heart to another, knowing that your well-being is out of your hands. Perhaps what I came to know more deeply was the absurd invitation to believe God is good when I have no idea about the outcome of any given day. I can't actually put words to what I sensed deep inside. All I know is that I shared something with my Father that forced me to choose to continue to trust His goodness.

After some days, I came to love Him even more for the sacrifice He had made to share our sorrow.

In Psalm 56:8, the psalmist writes, "You keep track of all my sorrows. You have collected all my tears in your bottle" (NLT). Our tears are treasured by our Father. I have been told that in biblical times, people treasured their tears as well, collecting them in a little cherished container. They were the heart of life. Sacred tears shed in sorrow mingled together with holy tears shed in joy, the alpha and omega of a life fully lived. Some scholars believe that when the woman barged into the Pharisee's home uninvited and wept at Jesus' feet, washing them with her tears, she may have poured her precious bottle of tears over him, symbolizing the totality of her life being offered.

Sometimes life feels too much to bear. And sometimes a distrust of God and His goodness is the fruit of sorrow. For me, the seeds of temptation to distrust the heart of God were planted in my grandson's grave. But we have a choice to make in the midst of overwhelming heartbreak. To hope or to despair. To be hardened by it or softened through it. To seek God in it or blame Him for it.

I was sitting with a friend in the warm afternoon sun one day while a pine-scented breeze gently moved the air. Her husband had died peacefully in their bed early that very morning. She had lain next to him all the long night before, stroking his hair, whispering love and tender endearments, using names they reserved only for one another. She was telling him, too, as it is so important to do, that it was okay for him to leave, that she was going to be all right. She told him that she knew she would see him again and, in the meantime, God would take care of her. She blessed his dying.

He took his last breath in her arms.

And she wept.

It had been nine hours, and she was gently weeping still. But she was not only weeping. She was intermittently telling stories, flowing into worship, slipping into prayer, and believing the words as she spoke them: "This is a new chapter in my life, and I know that God has good things for me."

Now, don't think for a moment that these were idle words coming from a woman who was not deeply attached to her husband. He was the love of her life. He still is. They met when she was sixteen years old, and nearly fifty years later they were just as committed to loving each other well as they were at the beginning.

Her words flowed from her heart, a heart that she continued to instruct to turn its gaze to Jesus. When she looked a little to the left or a smidge to the right, her heart plummeted into fear. But she recognized the shift immediately whenever she made it and then fixed her eyes on Jesus yet again, on the anchor of her soul. When she did, she could breathe in life, truth, hope, and comfort once more. All with tears streaming down her face.

Where is the defiant joy here? It is in the stance that says, "Death has not won." It lies in the choice of a heart that refuses to accuse God in the midst of sorrow. Defiant joy trusts. Defiant joy is expectant of good. And, in the case of my friend, defiant joy also invites several women over for a happy hour four days later to share stories, tears, and laughter. Sometimes loss is expressed in lament, and sometimes loss is expressed with inside jokes, but both are marked with wet cheeks.

Many of you know this sorrow. You know this loss. You've said goodbye to your parents, your spouse, your friend, your child.

I've said goodbye to both my parents, my father when I was twenty-three, my mother when I was forty. I've said goodbye to very close friends who've died suddenly in accidents and others who've died after long illnesses.

I have not known the pain of being parted from my child or my husband. I think of that, and I cannot breathe. I have not endured it, but those closest to my heart have.

I recently had the honor and the sorrow (yes, at the same time) of being at the memorial service for my friend Laura's twenty-four-year-old son, Jason. The service was holy. And I do mean *h.o.l.y.* We grieved his passing. Celebrated his life. Remained thankful for the truth that there is a happily ever after coming, when all will be restored. No more goodbyes. Ever.

I hate goodbyes.

But here's the thing.

At his service, nothing was shared about how Jason did or did not pick up his room. If he made his bed. Put his toys away. Nothing about how old he was when he was finally and fully potty-trained. Not a word about his grades, his degrees, or his titles. No one spoke of his weight or the size of his bank account.

Tons was shared, however, about how people felt in his presence. There were lots of stories about his sense of humor and how he came alive playing the drums and doing mission trips. Words flowed about how he loved people, how he lived passionately from his heart, and the joy he brought by simply being and offering his unique, quirky, imperfect, wonderful, on-the-road, beautiful self to everyone in his life.

It was his heart that mattered. And it's yours that matters. And it's also the hearts of all those who are left behind and have to endure the partings that matter. My friend Laura was living in the unchartered terrain of devastation at the loss of her youngest boy. Yes, he was a man, but in a mother's heart, though she sees and respects the man her son becomes, she continues to hold close the boy he once was. Laura's heart was broken, and from that very place she worshipped God. At her son's memorial service she stood and, with tears streaming, led worship. She exalted God. She proclaimed the truth. God is good. And she will be with her son again. As she sang, I witnessed a miracle of faith in the midst of a profound loss. I have been privileged to witness it many times.

As my Sam and his Susie buried their beloved son, Patrick Samuel, they read words proclaiming their love for him and their joy on his behalf that he was now safely home with Jesus, though he was home much too soon for their broken hearts. They missed him already. And they told him, speaking to themselves as much as to their first child, that they would miss him for their entire lives. Yet they knew that there was going to come a time, in only a little while, that they would embrace. They would play. They would trace his face with their fingers, tender with love. But they would have to wait. They would wait and they would long and they would never forget him. And in the waiting, they would be changed, transformed even more deeply to bear the face of love.

"By loss on loss, I have severely gained,"[2] George MacDonald wrote, and who of us cannot say that loss upon loss has characterized our lives as well?

This past year our family has known grief. We lost a brother, a grandson, and a best friend within months of each other. We experienced a betrayal from one we loved and trusted as well as a heavy blow in our ministry. We were blindsided by sorrow.

Grief attacks our belief in the goodness of God. Betrayal attacks the core of our identity. How did we not see it coming, we wonder? The death of a dream can put to death something in the soul as well. We are not alone in this.

But loss does not define us. There has been gain upon gain as well. Death does not win; it is actually the doorway to the resurrection. In time, if we will let it, the death of a dream will give birth to a honed vision. The death of a beloved deepens our souls and loosens our grip on treating this side of eternity as our final hope. It helps us hold dear the ones close to us, steeling our resolve, our choice, to risk love without restraint in the here and now. Our hearts rise up in an awakened state of sobriety about our lives.

Yes, we will miss those we have to say goodbye to. And yes, it is not only what the beloved brought to us and to others that we will miss. It is what they brought out of others and out of us that will be missed as well. They made us laugh as no one else could. They made us look at the world in a different light. They drew out from us a feeling of well-being that only they could draw. Their absence affects not only our life now but also our future lives and the person we may have become. Losing them affects everything.

C. S. Lewis wrote about this after he lost his beloved wife:

> Her absence is no more emphatic in those places than anywhere else. It's not local at all. I suppose if one were forbidden all salt one wouldn't notice it much more in any one food more than another. Eating in general would be different, every day, at every meal. It is like that. The act of living is different all through. Her absence is like the sky, spread over everything.[3]

Death renders a parting that is unimaginable. It is a goodbye that rings of finality like a bell sounding the end of all things. It is a goodbye that must be grieved. It is a parting not to be skipped over lightly with platitudes of "they're in a better place" or "it was God's will" or any other inane offering to smooth over the loss, regardless of how true it may be.

I know that our goodbyes here are temporary, but when someone we intimately love dies, it feels as if a huge part of us dies as well. Honestly, our lives will never be the same. One we love so deeply, who is engraved on our hearts, has gone on a long journey, and we cannot go with them. Not yet. Not yet. They are well, so we no longer have to worry about them, but they have gone out of our reach. They cannot contact us. We no longer share our lives with them. They won't be popping over for dinner. We will not hear their laugh for quite some time. They won't draw out from us that particular response that only they drew. We will see them again, be reunited forever—perhaps in a day, perhaps in a year—but until then, we will miss them.

And while we miss them, we will be forever changed by our loss. In the missing and the aching and the desperate pain, we will not give in to devastation. We are called to live. And eventually, miraculously, to live with joy.

The Sting

"Where, O death, is your victory? Where,
O death, is your sting?"
−1 CORINTHIANS 15:55

My friend Sue quoted the above verse, then pointed to her heart and said, "It [the sting] is right here." And then she broke down in tears, the pain flowing from the depths of her being. Her face crumpled in anguish. I know her sorrow. I share her pain. It is real. Currently the sting of death is coming in the loss of yet another we deeply love. The loss hurts with an intensity that is scorching, reminding us of every other goodbye we have had to say. Every memory of our shared life continues to rise to the surface, carrying both a gratitude and an ache that threaten to expand to the point that our hearts will explode from uncontainable grief. And explode they will.

Our hearts stretch to the bursting point in profound loss, don't they? They expand almost beyond bearing.

It is a sorrow that our Father knows well. It is a suffering that our Jesus would not spare us from. It is a pain that is born from loving.

I said goodbye to my cherished friend Craig yesterday. He is a man whom I have had the privilege of being loved by for more than thirty-five years. I hate cancer. I adore my friend.

Actually, I didn't say goodbye. On the islands of Hawaii, the locals never say it. They say *a hui hou* when they part from one another, which means "see you later." I guess that since they're living on an island, they know they will be running into each other again sooner or later. It is inevitable. But though I live on a large continent made of earth and water, dust and mud, beauty and heartbreak, I, too, said "I'll see you later" to my friend at our parting. Because I will.

The apostle Paul tells us in 1 Corinthians:

I declare to you, brothers and sisters, that flesh and blood cannot inherit the kingdom of God, nor does the perishable inherit the imperishable. Listen, I tell you a mystery: We will not all sleep, but we will all be changed—in a flash, in the twinkling of an eye, at the last trumpet. For the trumpet *will* sound, the dead *will* be raised imperishable, and we *will* be changed. . . . When the perishable has been clothed with the imperishable, and the mortal with immortality, then the saying that is written will come true: "Death has been swallowed up in victory." (1 Cor. 15:50–52, 54, emphasis added)

We will all be changed. We will live endlessly with our God and with one another, and we will rule and reign with Christ and enjoy Him forever. Partings are so painful, and the prospect of living out the rest of our days without the presence of ones we love is excruciating. But partings are *temporary*.

And so I rejoice. For my friend who has been freed from his suffering, I rejoice. For the victory that we have in Christ, I rejoice. For the truth of the coming kingdom, I rejoice. For the fact that I, and all those who put themselves in God's loving care, will one day pass into eternity and see our God face to face, and there will be no more tears and no more sorrow ever again, I rejoice. A grand and endless *hello* is coming.

I cling to the promise of the prophet Isaiah:

> And those the LORD has rescued will return.
> They will enter Zion with singing;
> everlasting joy will crown their heads.
> Gladness and joy will overtake them,
> and sorrow and sighing will flee away. (Isa. 35:10)

Roses

This morning I looked out my bedroom window and saw that the bushes I planted last summer have survived the harsh winter. This very day, my roses are bursting with pink buds, promising a full display of beauty and glory. Their stark branches had looked hopeless and defeated for many months. In the barren cold of winter, it appeared as if they would not survive, let alone bear their splendor ever again. But they have not only survived, they have expanded. Their roots have gone deep, and they have exploded with life. They are all that they are meant to be.

And so it will be, my friends. So it will be.

Sometimes I have wondered, *How can God be so joyful in the face of all the heartbreak in the world?* The answer is because He sees the great restoration as if it were already here.

All around us, gentle invitations of truth and grace call to us, if we will have the ears to hear. Today I do hear, and I am reminded of the promise of the restoration of all things. Death *has* lost its sting. The grave holds *no* victory. My visible world may scream loss, but the victory cannot and will not be held back. And because of that, because life wins and has won already, because of all Jesus has won for us, I—like you—can be defiantly joyful. I will choose it. Join me.

A hui hou.

Daily Prayers

Prayer to Receive Jesus as Savior

The most important relationship for every one of us is our relationship with Jesus Christ. Choosing to believe that He is who He claimed to be—the Son of God and the only way to salvation—and receiving Him by faith as your Lord and Savior is the most vital act anyone will ever do. We want life. He is Life. We need cleansing. He is the Living Water.

Here is a simple prayer if you have not yet given your life to Jesus and invited Him into yours:

Jesus, I believe You are the Son of God, that You died on the cross to rescue me from sin and death and to restore me to the Father. I choose now to turn from my sins, my self-centeredness, and every part of my life that does not please You. I choose You. I give myself to You. I receive Your forgiveness and ask You to take

Your rightful place in my life as my Savior and Lord. Come reign in my heart, fill me with Your love and Your life, and help me to become a person who is truly loving—a person like You. Restore me, Jesus. Live in me. Love through me. Thank You, God. In Jesus' name I pray, amen.

Saint Patrick's Breastplate

I arise today
Through a mighty strength, the invocation of the
    Trinity,
Through belief in the Threeness,
Through confession of the Oneness
of the Creator of creation.

I arise today
Through the strength of Christ's birth with His
    baptism,
Through the strength of His crucifixion with His burial,
Through the strength of His resurrection with His
    ascension,
Through the strength of His descent for the
    judgment of doom.

I arise today
Through the strength of the love of cherubim,

In the obedience of angels,

In the service of archangels,

In the hope of resurrection to meet with reward,

In the prayers of patriarchs,

In the predictions of prophets,

In the preaching of apostles,

In the faith of confessors,

In the innocence of holy virgins,

In the deeds of righteous men.

I arise today, through

The strength of heaven,

The light of the sun,

The radiance of the moon,

The splendor of fire,

The speed of lightning,

The swiftness of wind,

The depth of the sea,

The stability of the earth,

The firmness of rock.

I arise today, through

God's strength to pilot me,

God's might to uphold me,

God's wisdom to guide me,

God's eye to look before me,

God's ear to hear me,

God's word to speak for me,

God's hand to guard me,
God's shield to protect me,
God's host to save me
From snares of devils,
From temptation of vices,
From everyone who shall wish me ill,
afar and near.

I summon today
All these powers between me and those evils,
Against every cruel and merciless power
that may oppose my body and soul,
Against incantations of false prophets,
Against black laws of pagandom,
Against false laws of heretics,
Against craft of idolatry,
Against spells of witches and smiths and wizards,
Against every knowledge that corrupts man's body
    and soul;
Christ to shield me today
Against poison, against burning,
Against drowning, against wounding,
So that there may come to me an abundance of
    reward.

Christ with me,
Christ before me,
Christ behind me,

Christ in me,

Christ beneath me,

Christ above me,

Christ on my right,

Christ on my left,

Christ when I lie down,

Christ when I sit down,

Christ when I arise,

Christ in the heart of every man who thinks of me,

Christ in the mouth of everyone who speaks of me,

Christ in every eye that sees me,

Christ in every ear that hears me.

Daily Prayers

My dear Lord Jesus, I come to You now to be restored in You, renewed in You, to receive Your life and Your love and all the grace and mercy I so desperately need this day. I honor You as my Lord, and I surrender every aspect and dimension of my life to You. I give You my spirit, soul, and body, my heart, mind, and will. I cover myself with Your blood—my spirit, soul, and body, my heart, mind, and will. I ask Your Holy Spirit to restore me in You, renew me in You, and lead this time of prayer. In all that I now pray, I stand in total agreement with Your Spirit and with all those praying for me by the Spirit of God and by the Spirit of God alone.

Dearest God, holy and victorious Trinity, You alone are worthy of all my worship, my heart's devotion, all my praise, all my trust, and all the glory of my life. I love You, I worship You, I give myself over to You in my heart's search for life. You alone are Life, and You have become my life. I renounce all other gods, every idol, and I give to You, God, the place in my heart and in my life that You truly deserve. This is all about You, and not about me. You are the Hero of this story, and I belong to You. I ask Your forgiveness for my every sin. Search me, know me, and reveal to me where You are working in my life, and grant to me the grace of Your healing and deliverance and a deep and true repentance.

Heavenly Father, thank You for loving me and choosing me before You made the world. You are my true Father—my creator, redeemer, sustainer, and the true end of all things, including my life. I love You, I trust You, I worship You. I give myself over to You, Father, to be one with You as Jesus is one with You. Thank You for proving Your love for me by sending Jesus. I receive Him and all His life and all His work which You ordained for me. Thank You for including me in Christ, forgiving me my sins, granting me His righteousness, making me complete in Him. Thank You for making me alive with Christ, raising me with Him, seating me with Him at your right hand, establishing me in His

*authority, and anointing me with Your love and Your
Spirit and Your favor. I receive it all with thanks and
give it total claim to my life—my spirit, soul, and body,
my heart, mind, and will.*

*Jesus, thank You for coming to ransom me with Your
own life. I love You, worship You, trust You. I give myself
over to You to be one with You in all things. I receive
all the work and triumph of Your cross, death, blood,
and sacrifice for me, through which my every sin is
atoned for, I am ransomed, delivered from the kingdom of darkness, and transferred to Your kingdom; my
sin nature is removed, my heart circumcised unto God,
and every claim being made against me is cancelled
and disarmed. I take my place now in Your cross and
death, dying with You to sin, to my flesh, to this world,
to the evil one and his kingdom. I take up the cross
and crucify my flesh with all its pride, arrogance, unbelief, and idolatry [and anything else you are currently struggling with]. I put off the old man. Apply
to me all the work and triumph in Your cross, death,
blood, and sacrifice; I receive it with thanks and give
it total claim to my spirit, soul, and body, my heart,
mind, and will.*

*Jesus, I also receive You as my Life, and I receive all the
work and triumph in Your resurrection, through which
You have conquered sin, death, judgment, and the evil*

one. Death has no power over You, nor does any foul thing. And I have been raised with You to a new life, to live Your life—dead to sin and alive to God. I take my place now in Your resurrection and in Your life, and I give my life to You to live Your life. I am saved by Your life. I reign in life through Your life. I receive Your hope, love, faith, joy, goodness, trueness, wisdom, power, and strength. Apply to me all the work and triumph in Your resurrection; I receive it with thanks, and I give it total claim to my spirit, soul, and body, my heart, mind, and will.

Jesus, I also sincerely receive You as my authority, rule, and dominion, my everlasting victory against Satan and his kingdom, and my ability to bring Your kingdom at all times and in every way. I receive all the work and triumph in Your ascension, through which Satan has been judged and cast down. All authority in the heavens and on this earth has been given to You, Jesus, and You are worthy to receive all glory and honor, power and dominion, now and forever. I take my place now in Your authority and in Your throne, through which I have been raised with You to the right hand of the Father and established in Your authority. I give myself to You, to reign with You always. Apply to me all the work and triumph in Your authority and Your throne; I receive it with thanks and I give it total claim to my spirit, soul, and body, my heart, mind, and will.

I now bring the authority, rule, and dominion of the Lord Jesus Christ and the full work of Christ over my life today: over my home, my household, my work, over all my kingdom and domain. I bring the authority of the Lord Jesus Christ and the full work of Christ against every evil power coming against me—against every foul spirit, every foul power and device. [You might need to name them—what has been attacking you?] I cut them off in the name of the Lord; I bind and banish them from me and from my kingdom now, in the mighty name of Jesus Christ. I also bring the full work of Christ between me and every person, and I allow only the love of God and only the Spirit of God between us.

Holy Spirit, thank You for coming. I love You, I worship You, I trust You. I receive all the work and triumph in Pentecost, through which You have come. You have clothed me with power from on high, sealed me in Christ, become my union with the Father and the Son, the Spirit of truth in me, the life of God in me, my counselor, comforter, strength, and guide. I honor You as Lord, and I fully give to You every aspect and dimension of my spirit, soul, and body, my heart, mind, and will—to be filled with You, to walk in step with you in all things. Fill me afresh, Holy Spirit. Restore my union with the Father and the Son. Lead me into all truth, anoint me for all of my life and walk and calling, and lead me deeper into Jesus today. I receive You with thanks, and I give You total claim to my life.

Heavenly Father, thank You for granting to me every spiritual blessing in Christ Jesus. I claim the riches in Christ Jesus over my life today. I bring the blood of Christ once more over my spirit, soul, and body, over my heart, mind, and will. I put on the full armor of God: the belt of truth, breastplate of righteousness, shoes of the gospel, helmet of salvation. I take up the shield of faith and sword of the Spirit, and I choose to be strong in the Lord and in the strength of Your might, to pray at all times in the Spirit.

Jesus, thank You for your angels. I summon them in the name of Jesus Christ and instruct them to destroy all that is raised against me, to establish Your kingdom over me, to guard me day and night. I ask You to send forth Your Spirit to raise up prayer and intercession for me. I now call forth the kingdom of God throughout my home, my household, my kingdom, and my domain in the authority of the Lord Jesus Christ, giving all glory and honor and thanks to Him. In Jesus' name, amen.

Acknowledgments

No creative work is ever done alone. This book, *Defiant Joy*, is the fruit of a life lived in the company of others who hold fast to the truths that the best is yet to come and that they are safely and forever held in the love of God. Family, friends, and allies of Ransomed Heart help me daily to remember that within every moment of life there remains a reason for joy.

My agent and his *ezer* wife, Curtis and Karen Yates, make quite the team. Thank you both for your eyes, your skill, your gifts, your passionate faith, your commitment to Jesus, and your belief in me. I am so grateful. Hooray for Yates & Yates!

My editor, Jessica Wong, was committed to helping me make this manuscript the best it could be, and I am so grateful for her hard work. Also, special thanks goes out to the copyeditors, Brigitta Nortker and Karin Silver, for their deft touches. In fact, to the entire team at Thomas Nelson, I stand

and applaud you. It's been a great good to partner with you in every aspect of this book. Thank you.

To my friends who spur me on, I am forever grateful. I want to particularly thank Carrie Hayner, Sue Rowland, Sallie Ross, Laura Mastroianni, Becky Allender, and Lori McConnell. These women are champions and they champion me. I love doing life with you.

I am beyond words grateful for my ministry compatriots at Ransomed Heart: men and women who are of the finest caliber. They love God passionately and live with a true joy that is deep, rich, and authentic. Allen Arnold, thank you especially for your continual offerings of wisdom and encouragement regarding this project. Those fabulous qualities bless me beyond measure and are shared by all the saints that surround me there—Brad and Lisa Beck, Morgan and Cherie Snyder, Jamie Goudie, Stacey Burton, Alex Burton, Polly Belloso, Jon Dale, Justin Lukasavige, Julie Musilli, Karen Christakis, Sam Ainslie, and Bart Hansen—you are all stellar, and I'm so thankful for all you have poured and continue to pour into my life. Cheers.

My sisters and brother, Terri, Kelly, and Jim, were my first entrance into laughter in the face of goodness and the not quite so nice. Forever we will burst into song at "I heard the voice of a lonely Mexican maiden." They would take a bullet for me and I for them. They cheer for me, and I am so grateful. I love you.

To my beloved family: Sam, Susie, Finley, Button, Blaine, Emilie, Eilish, Luke, and Olivia—I am truly the most blessed and richest woman indeed to have such amazing ones to love and be loved by. You make my heart burst. Sharing life with you is the highest privilege, and I thank God for you every single day. You are my treasures. *You* are my joys.

And then there's this man that I am privileged to love. He's my hero, my best friend, my advocate, my warrior, my lover, the champion of my heart, and happily, my husband. This book would not be possible without John. He has encouraged me, taught me, and led the way before me into every good, beautiful, and holy place I have come to know and enjoy. It's my name on the cover, but his should be there too.

This book was written in a partnership between Jesus and me. I wrote from a heart that is so very thankful for His unending, masterful, unyielding, and extravagant love. We did it together *for you*, dear reader, and I am so very thankful for the places God and I went in my heart as I wrote. So thank *you*.

About the Author

Stasi Eldredge is a *New York Times* bestselling author, and her books have sold nearly 3 million copies and changed women's lives all over the world. A teacher and conference speaker, Stasi is the director of the women's ministry at Ransomed Heart, a ministry devoted to helping people discover the heart of God, recover their own hearts in God's love, and learn to live in God's kingdom. Her passion is to see lives transformed by the beauty of the gospel. She and her husband, John, make their home in Colorado Springs, Colorado.

Notes

Introduction
1. Philippians 4:4, author's paraphrase.

Chapter 1: A Holy Defiance
1. "Sandy Hook Shooting: What Happened?" CNN, December 2012, http://www.cnn.com/interactive/2012/12/us/sandy -hook-timeline/index.html.
2. Meister Eckhart, *Meditations with Meister Eckhart*, trans. and ed. Matthew Fox (Rochester, VT: Bear, 1983), 129.

Chapter 2: The Cup
1. Charles Dickens, *A Tale of Two Cities* (London: Chapman and Hall, 1859), 7.
2. Brent Curtis and John Eldredge, *The Sacred Romance* (Nashville: Thomas Nelson, 1997), 133.
3. Brian Tabb, "Rejoice Even Though: Facing the Challenges to Joy," Desiring God, October 16, 2016, https://www .desiringgod.org/articles/rejoice-even-though.
4. Brian Hardin, *Sneezing Jesus: How God Redeems Our Humanity* (Colorado Springs: NavPress, 2017), 102.
5. "Holy Eucharist II," in *The Book of Common Prayer* (New York: Church Hymnal Corporation, 2007), 338. Available

online at the (Online) Book of Common Prayer, last modified December 15, 2016, https://www.bcponline.org/.

Chapter 3: Whiplash

1. John Eldredge, *Walking with God: Talk to Him, Hear from Him, Really* (Nashville: Thomas Nelson, 2008).
2. "St. Patrick's Breastplate," Our Catholic Prayers, last modified 2018, http://www.ourcatholicprayers.com/st-patricks -breastplate.html.
3. "St. Patrick's Breastplate."
4. "St. Patrick's Breastplate."
5. "St. Patrick's Breastplate."

Chapter 4: Interference

1. Alicia VanOrman and Beth Jarosz, "Suicide Replaces Homicide as Second-Leading Cause of Death Among U.S. Teenagers," Population Reference Bureau, June 2016, http://www.prb.org /Publications/Articles/2016/suicide-replaces-homicide-second -leading-cause-death-among-us-teens.aspx; Emily Thomas, "Suicide Among Young Veterans Rising at Alarming Rate," *Huffington Post*, January 10, 2014, http://www.huffingtonpost .com/2014/01/10/young-veteran-suicide-doubles_n_4576846 .html.
2. Dan Allender, *The Wounded Heart: Hope for Adult Victims of Childhood Sexual Abuse* (Colorado Springs: NavPress, 2008), 199.

Chapter 5: Greener Grass

1. Dan Allender, *To Be Told: God Invites You to Coauthor Your Future* (Colorado Springs: WaterBrook, 2005).
2. C. S. Lewis, *The Weight of Glory* (New York: HarperOne, 1980), 141.
3. Ann Voskamp, as posted by Chelsea Patterson, "Dear You . . . A Letter for All of the Hard Days," *Joy Indestructible* (blog),

September 30, 2014, http://www.patheos.com/blogs
/joyindestructible/2014/09/30/dear-you-a-letter-for-the
-hard-days/.

Chapter 6: A Divine Exchange
1. Becky Allender, *Hidden in Plain Sight* (Bainbridge Island, WA: Blue Wing Press, 2017), 10.
2. Wendell Berry, *The Art of the Commonplace: The Agrarian Essays* (Berkeley, CA: Counterpoint, 2002), 311.

Chapter 7: Expectant
1. John 16:33, author's paraphrase.
2. Graham Cooke, "Joy Is Who God Is," *Brilliant Perspectives* (blog), accessed February 20, 2018, http://brilliantperspectives. com/joy-is-who-god-is/. The quote is excerpted from Cooke's book, *Approaching the Heart of Prophecy: A Journey into Encouragement, Blessing, and Prophetic Gifting* (Winston-Salem, NC: Punch Press, 2006).
3. George MacDonald, "May," in *A Book of Strife in the Form of the Diary of an Old Soul* (London: Mr. Hughes, 1880), 103, 105.

Chapter 8: Thieves That Come
1. Adapted from Lewis's comment on fellow Inkling J. R. R. Tolkien's book *The Fellowship of the Ring*: "This book is lightning from a clear sky." Quoted in Douglas Gilbert and Clyde S. Kilby, *C. S. Lewis: Images of His World* (Grand Rapids: Eerdmans, 2005), 52.
2. Brené Brown, *The Gifts of Imperfection: Let Go of Who You Think You're Supposed to Be and Embrace Who You Are* (Center City, MN: Hazelden, 2010), 82.
3. English by *Oxford Dictionaries*, s.v. "dread," accessed February 20, 2018, https://en.oxforddictionaries.com/definition/dread.
4. Sarah Young, *Jesus Always: Embracing Joy in His Presence* (Nashville: Thomas Nelson, 2016), May 18 reading.

5. In communication with the author, July 2017, emphasis added. Used by permission.

Chapter 9: The Signs All Around Us

1. Joni Mitchell (lyricist and performer), "Big Yellow Taxi," from *Ladies of the Canyon*, released 1970. Lyrics at "Big Yellow Taxi," Joni Mitchell.com, accessed February 27, 2018, http://jonimitchell.com/music/song.cfm?id=13.
2. George MacDonald, *Phantastes* (London: Smith, Elder, and Co., 1858), 322, author's paraphrase.
3. Sarah Young, *Jesus Calling: Enjoying Peace in His Presence* (Nashville: Thomas Nelson, 2004), February 5 reading.
4. "Brain Post: How Much Time Does the Average American Spend Indoors?" *SnowBrains* (blog), May 1, 2018, https://snowbrains.com/brain-post-much-time-average-american-spend-outdoors/.
5. Jared Newnam, "Spending Time in Nature for Your Health— How Outdoor Activities Improve Well-Being," South University Blog, September 6, 2012, https://www.southuniversity.edu/whoweare/newsroom/blog/spending-time-in-nature-for-your-health-how-outdoor-activities-improve-wellbeing-102984.
6. John Eldredge and Stasi Eldredge, *Love and War: Find Your Way to Something Beautiful in Your Marriage* (Colorado Springs: WaterBrook, 2009), 70–71.

Chapter 10: Cultivating Joy

1. Sarah Young, *Jesus Calling: Enjoying Peace in His Presence* (Nashville: Thomas Nelson, 2004), July 24 reading.
2. John Eldredge, *All Things New: Heaven, Earth, and the Restoration of Everything You Love* (Nashville: Thomas Nelson, 2017), 91. Emphasis in the original.
3. C. S. Lewis, *The Last Battle* (1956; New York: HarperCollins, 2002), 230.

4. George MacDonald, "Within and Without" in *The Poetical Works of George MacDonald*, vol.1 (London: Chatto & Windus, 1893), 83.

5. Ann Voskamp, *One Thousand Gifts: A Dare to Live Fully Right Where You Are* (Grand Rapids: Zondervan, 2010), 139.

6. Arthur C. Brooks, "Choose to Be Grateful. It Will Make You Happier," *New York Times*, November 22, 2015, https://www.nytimes.com/2015/11/22/opinion/sunday/choose-to-be-grateful-it-will-make-you-happier.html. The original study cited in the article: Roland Zahn et. al, "The Neural Basis of Human Social Values: Evidence from Functional MRI," *Cerebral Cortex* 19, no. 2 (2009): 276–83.

7. Voskamp, *One Thousand Gifts*, 35. Emphasis in original.

Chapter 11: On Behalf of Love

1. Tim Perone, "Heroic Teachers Made the Ultimate Sacrifice for Kids," *New York Post*, December 16, 2012, https://nypost.com/2012/12/16/heroic-teachers-made-the-ultimate-sacrifice-for-kids/.

2. Bill Gaultiere, "Four Degrees of Love (Bernard of Clairvaux)," *Soul Shepherding* (blog), August 19, 2013, http://www.soulshepherding.org/2013/08/bernard-of-clairvauxs-four-degrees-of-love/. The full text of Bernard of Clairvaux's book is available online at Christian Classics Ethereal Library, http://www.ccel.org/ccel/bernard/loving_god.html.

3. Bernard of Clairvaux, *On Loving God* (Shawnee, KS: Gideon House Books), chap. 9.

4. Clairvaux, *On Loving God*.

5. Bernard of Clairvaux (1090–1153), "Jesus, the Very Thought of Thee," trans. Edward Caswall, lyrics available at Timeless Truths, http://library.timelesstruths.org/music/Jesus_the_Very_Thought_of_Thee/.

6. Clairvaux, *On Loving God*, chap. 10.

7. Dennis Prager, "Happiness Is a Moral Obligation,"

DennisPrager.com, February 20, 2007, http://www
.dennisprager.com/happiness-is-a-moral-obligation/.

8. Hardin, *Sneezing Jesus*, 39 (see chap. 2, n. 4).

Chapter 12: A Hui Hou

1. Wikipedia, s.v. "Origins of the Blues," last modified February
20, 2018, https://en.wikipedia.org/wiki/Origins_of_the_blues;
Guido Fackler, "Music in Concentration Camps 1933–1945,"
Music & Politics 1, no. 1 (2007), available online at University
of Michigan Library, https://quod.lib.umich.edu/m/mp
/9460447.0001.102/--music-in-concentration-camps-1933–
1945?rgn=main;view=fulltext.

2. MacDonald, "May," in *A Book of Strife*, 109 (see chap. 7, n. 3).

3. C. S. Lewis, *A Grief Observed* (1961; New York:
HarperCollins, 1994), 11.

New Video Study for Your Church or Small Group

If you've enjoyed this book, now you can go deeper with the companion video Bible study!

In this 6-session study, Stasi Eldredge helps you apply the principles in *Defiant Joy* to your life. The study guide includes video notes, group discussion questions, and personal study and reflection materials for in-between sessions.

Study Guide
9780310096900

DVD
9780310096924

Available now at your favorite bookstore, or streaming video on StudyGateway.com.